Double Take
Karen Brain's Olympic Journey

Double Take

Karen Brain's Olympic Journey

NIKKI TATE

sononis
PRESS
WINLAW, BRITISH COLUMBIA

For Merlin

Copyright © 2007 by Nikki Tate

Library and Archives Canada Cataloguing in Publication

Tate, Nikki, 1962-
  Double take : Karen Brain's olympic journey / Nikki Tate.

Includes index.
ISBN 978-1-55039-162-6

  1. Brain, Karen. 2. Dressage riders—Canada—Biography.
3. Paralympics. 4. Horsemen and horsewomen—Canada—Biography.
5. Athletes with disabilities—Canada—Biography. I. Title.

SF309.482.B73T38 2007   798.2092   C2007-904644-4

Sono Nis Press most gratefully acknowledges support for our publishing program provided by the Government of Canada through the Book Publishing Industry Development Program (BPIDP) and the Canada Council for the Arts, and by the Province of British Columbia through the British Columbia Arts Council and the Book Publishing Tax Credit, Ministry of Provincial Revenue.

All photography by Darlene Brain unless otherwise noted.
Front cover image of Karen Brain and VDL Odette by Danielle Tate-Stratton.

Edited by Dawn Loewen and Laura Peetoom
Proofread by Audrey McClellan
Cover and interior design by Patrice Snopkowski, OutWest Design

Published by
SONO NIS PRESS
Box 160
Winlaw, BC V0G 2J0

1-800-370-5228
1-250-226-0077

books@sononis.com
www.sononis.com

Distributed in the U.S. by
Orca Book Publishers
Box 468
Custer, WA 98240-0468

1-800-210-5277

Printed and bound in Canada by Friesens Printing.
Printed on acid-free paper that is forest friendly (100% post-consumer recycled paper) that has been processed chlorine free.

The Canada Council | Le Conseil des Arts
for the Arts | du Canada

Contents

Foreword

WHEN NIKKI AND I FIRST SAT DOWN and discussed her writing my biography, I was of course honoured as well as excited at the prospect. We had been friends for many years by then, and I had already been honoured with a dedication in her book *Jessa Be Nimble, Rebel Be Quick* in 1998. I had full trust in Nikki's ability not only to create an accurate account of my more momentous events up to now, but to capture the heartfelt emotions of those events as well.

In the many hours we spent together researching this book, Nikki taking notes and recordings while I rambled on about all my adventures, it soon became clear to me what this book meant to me personally. While reminiscing through my years, not only did I fondly relive all those special moments; I also relived every emotion associated with them. Poor Nikki. While she may have needed her own box of tissues for allergies during these visits, she probably wasn't prepared for the "Brain waterworks" that would require a box of tissues all on their own! It seems whether the memories were extremely happy and joyous or sad and poignant, I was moved to tears regardless.

It is at this point that I want to say a huge thank you to my dear mother for all her tireless hours searching for pictures, childhood memorabilia, baby books, and all the articles used to compile this book. She was a godsend, and had Nikki had only me to rely on, well, this book might have never seen its finished form. But aside from the practical input Mom had, I want to also thank her for sharing in the wonderful and sad stories all over again with me. As we shared tears, laughs, jokes, and then more tears, I felt a cathartic healing overcome me. I am truly blessed with an amazing mom and dad, and it is because of them that I was able to do all of what you are about to read.

Another very special mention must go to the namesake of this book, Double Take. Just ask Nikki: whenever she asked me any questions about Double Take, a.k.a. Merlin, it quickly became another tissue moment! Merlin is my pride and joy and carries a heart the size of Texas in his smallish 15.3 hh body. He was a source of great frustration during our earlier years together, only to become the pinnacle of my competitive career years later. He is in character much of what I strive to become: authentic, generous hearted, trusting, forgiving, and forever childlike in enthusiasm. Without Merlin my life would have been only a puddle of memories compared to the sea of experiences I've had. I am eternally grateful to him for all that he has given me. He is a true kindred soul and I am honoured to have been able to "soar like an eagle" upon his back. Thank you, Merlin! And thank you, Dani, for suggesting the perfect title for this book.

It is a funny thing being asked about your childhood experiences and the details of events that you realize are already half forgotten. It makes you delve a little deeper into the truth of each situation and leaves you asking yourself what you learned having gone through it. It was during the quieter moments by myself after Nikki's visits that I reflected on those questions and on ideas for this foreword.

I have said it many times to many people: I honestly do consider myself one of the luckiest people I know. More and more as I age, I catch myself saying, "Everything always works out for me in the end," and that is the truth. I have experienced dreams come true and many personal goals attained. I have been blessed with a great family, great friends, and several great horses, and it is because of all of them that I have lived a rich life.

Of course, you will quickly learn that not all was "peaches and cream" throughout these years. I had my fair share of stumbling blocks, difficulties, and falls along the way! I have cried over having my heart broken, just as I have felt great remorse for hurting someone I love. I have felt regret, just as I have felt anger. Yet the most character-building lessons came not from the easy days, but from the hardest of hard days. And while I am not a glutton for punishment, I also cannot ignore the fact that those hard times did in fact end up being good for me.

I believe that whether someone is a best friend or is perceived as a worst enemy, they are here to help teach us, just as we are here to help them learn. I owe thanks to all who have been a part of my life, whether that part was long and meaningful or short and awkward. All have helped make me who I am today.

And so, from my most beloved kindred spirits to the sixth grader who picked on me after school, I thank you. From the boys who broke my heart to those who taught me to be true to myself, I thank you. From the dear friend who told me lovingly something very hard to hear, to those who too easily said much that wasn't worth hearing, I thank you. From the strangers who left me inspirational notes on my tack box during bleak moments, to those who put obstacles in my way, I thank you. From the horses who were a breeze to train, to the rebellious one who fundamentally changed my life's path, I thank you.

As you read Nikki's delightful recounting of my life's adventures, I encourage you to think about how your own biography might read one day. Start creating the memories for each chapter today by daring to live out your most heartfelt fantasies. If you can dream it, you can do it!

God bless, and enjoy the book!

Karen Brain,
Victoria, B.C., June 25, 2007

Acknowledgements

THIS BOOK WOULD NOT HAVE BEEN POSSIBLE without the generous cooperation of Karen Brain and her family. Not only did Karen, Darlene, and Bill welcome me into their home (where I was always well fed and coffeed), but they also gave me hours and hours of time, a precious commodity in our busy world. They opened the family scrapbooks, bundles of letters, and boxes of photographs and entrusted me with their contents. And they opened their hearts, sharing stories that were by turn funny, tragic, inspiring, surprising, and hopeful. This remarkable family shared triumphs and disappointments with such grace and honesty that I was constantly reminded of the great responsibility with which I was being entrusted: to tell another's story fairly and well. Whatever errors or misinterpretations may appear in the book are all mine. I only hope there aren't too many and that those that may have slipped in are not grave.

Thanks, too, to my editors Laura Peetoom and Dawn Loewen, who have helped shape the story from the very beginning. The book would not look as good as it does without the fine design work of Patrice Snopkowski—thank you! Dani, you did a sterling job as my assistant—I hope you have recovered from your never-ending scanathon. Diane Morriss of Sono Nis Press supported this project from the very beginning, and I cannot say how much I appreciate her stalwart support of my writing endeavours.

Perhaps the biggest thanks of all go to you, the reader, for picking up this book. I hope you find Karen's amazing story as inspiring as I do!

Introduction

At the end of grade five (1980), here's what Karen had to say about her plans for the future:

Karen Brain
    Karen has one sister and 27 pets of all kinds. Karen is
good at horse back riding, music and track and field which are
her hobbies. She wants to be an Olympic Equestrian rider and a
secretary. She says she doesn't have a boyfriend but who would
believe that story. Her best friend is Laura Hatt and her favourite saying is, "Just get lost why don't you". She hangs out at
the stables.

Olympic Dreams

In the back seat of the car, nine-year-old Karen Brain closes her eyes and holds her hands out in front of her. Her fingers curl around an imaginary pair of reins, and her boot heels twitch as she steers an invisible horse around a course of huge jumps. As clearly as if it's booming from huge speakers right in the back of the car, the deep voice of the announcer says, "Quiet, please, ladies and gentlemen. One more clean jump and Karen Brain of Canada will win her first Olympic gold medal."

Oblivious to her sister in the back seat beside her, the music playing on the radio, or the other traffic driving along the Pat Bay Highway north of Victoria, British Columbia, Karen drives her heels into her imaginary horse's sides and urges him to jump higher than he ever has before.

The horse responds, gathering himself beneath her, punching off the ground with his hind legs. They soar into the air and Karen knows they will clear the red and white rails below. Karen reaches forward to pat the show jumper's sweat-slicked neck as they land. The crowd roars and Karen hears the announcer say, "A tremendous effort! A wonderful gold medal ride!"

"Karen? Did you hear me?" Darlene Brain interrupts her younger daughter's daydream. "I have to run a few errands, but I'll be back to watch the end of your riding lesson."

Karen nods, already wrenching the car door open. She bolts toward the ring, barely hearing her mother call out, "Have fun, girls!"

As a young child, Karen Brain had a dream: to win medals riding horses at the Olympic Games. Many children love to ride, and lots of young riders dream of someday riding in the Olympics. But to Karen, her dream felt more like a plan. The facts may have been stacked against her—her family didn't have a lot of money, Karen didn't own a horse, and she could barely stay aboard during her early riding lessons—but Karen was undeterred. Deep in her heart, Karen *knew* that one day she would ride at the Olympics. Not only that, she would win a medal. She could not imagine any other future for herself.

Getting to the Olympic Games in an equestrian sport takes more than just willpower, though a rider needs plenty of that, too. For one thing, a rider needs a good horse—and buying, training, and looking after a horse costs a lot of money. Riders commit countless hours to training with their horses. There are several equestrian disciplines at the Olympic Games, but

Karen and Double Take (Merlin) on the cross-country course in Lumby, British Columbia, in 1994.

one of the most demanding is eventing. Riders who choose this challenging sport must excel in three areas: dressage, cross-country jumping, and stadium jumping.

Riders need to do well at international competitions to prove they belong on Canada's national team. Getting a rider and horse to an event in Europe easily costs more than twenty thousand dollars, and the time it takes to prepare for high-level competition is measured in months and years, not days and weeks.

Finally, a rider needs a bit of luck: luck that a horse produces its best-ever dressage score at an Olympic qualifying event; luck in finding a sponsor willing to bring a horse and rider together and help cover their expenses; luck in keeping all the rails up during a critical show jumping round.

What happens when luck turns against you? What if your brilliant jumper suffers a career-ending injury just before the Olympics? What if the young horse you are riding falls on top of you during a training ride? What if you break your back and find yourself partially paralyzed from the waist down? Do you give up on your dreams of winning an Olympic medal and find something else to occupy your time?

Not if your name is Karen Brain.

Eleven days before this photo was taken in 2001, Karen's horse fell on her and broke her back, leaving her an incomplete paraplegic. Here, Karen and her father wait outside the hospital for Rob Close to arrive with the horse trailer and Karen's horses, Merlin and Miko.

1

A Rider in the Making

First Lessons

"ME, TOO!"

Eight-year-old Karen Brain was not staying at home while her older sister, Terri, went to Oak Meadows farm for a riding lesson. Darlene Brain knew better than to take on her determined younger daughter, who was already pulling on her shiny new silver jacket. Karen wanted to look cool at her first riding lesson.

Despite Karen's enthusiasm, her first lesson, on a pony called Muffet, wasn't exactly the exciting ride she had expected. The constant stream of instructions was confusing.

"Keep your heels down!"

"Don't let your elbows flap!"

"Your reins are too loose!"

Each time Karen adjusted one thing, she forgot about something else. The first time Muffet trotted, the pony's short, choppy strides made Karen's teeth clack together and her head feel as if it was going to bob right off her neck.

It didn't matter. All the way home from the barn, Karen imagined herself galloping around the ring on Muffet, soaring over jumps far bigger than anyone would expect. Though she had enjoyed a few trail rides when she was younger, that first riding lesson sparked a serious obsession. Before that, Karen confesses, "My favourite animals were whales, dolphins, and rabbits. I had rabbits when I was very little, but I couldn't ride them! When I realized how much fun riding was, I lost interest in the bunnies pretty fast."

Each week, Karen and Terri rode in a group lesson taught by Trudy Madson. The riders practised steering and learned to make their horses walk, trot, and canter. One day, Trudy asked the riders to practise their two-point position. She explained how the students had to stand up in their stirrups, raising their bottoms out of their saddles and resting their hands on their mounts' necks. Karen had never tried to stand up in her stirrups while Muffet was moving; the manoeuvre was much harder than it looked. She leaned forward and straightened her legs completely until she was standing way up out of the saddle. Karen felt as if she were about to ride in the Kentucky Derby!

After showing Karen how to keep her knees bent and her body in a more balanced position, Trudy asked if she'd like to try a jump.

Karen was thrilled. Muffet trotted to the cavaletti and hopped over. Karen's reins were loose and she fell forward on

Despite losing her stirrups, Karen manages to stay on when her pony, Muffet, hops over a cavaletti in a riding lesson in 1978.

the pony's neck. She pushed herself back into the saddle and winced inwardly. Karen knew it hadn't been a great jump, but she had survived without crashing, and she was determined to do better next time.

The following week, the cavaletti had been replaced with a small course of low fences. Karen was excited, but her mouth was dry and her hands were unsteady on the reins. She swallowed hard and started to ride, knowing she was supposed to find a straight-line approach to the first jump. Karen urged Muffet forward and then, hypnotized by the jump, she did all the things she wasn't supposed to do. Instead of looking through her pony's ears to a point over and beyond the fence, she looked right down at it. She forgot to keep encouraging Muffet to move forward so they'd have enough momentum to clear the fence. Muffet, sensing her rider's insecurity, ducked out at the last second, throwing Karen half out of the saddle. Barely clinging on, Karen teetered sideways as Muffet raced toward a completely different fence!

Terrified, Karen prayed the pony would stop before launching herself over the coop jump. Totally out of control, the pony galloped toward the fence and then hit the brakes right at the last moment. Karen fell forward onto her pony's neck and then slid off into the dirt, landing with a thump.

The experience gave her a good scare, and she worried. How was she ever going to get to the Olympics if she fell off at such a tiny fence? Karen shook her head when her teacher asked if she wanted to try again. Instead, she joined the others in the line at the side of the ring and watched as, one after the other, her classmates cleared the coop jump. Nobody else fell off. All the others rode better than she did and she hated how that made her feel. Even worse, to Karen, had been the feeling of completely losing control.

Karen and her cousin Jenny Howard ride double on Cherokee outside Karen's house, 1981. Author's note: Riding double is not safe and isn't recommended, and an approved riding helmet should always be worn when mounted.

Cherokee

By age nine, Karen was working at a barn owned by Carol Webster. She swept up, mucked out stalls, and scrubbed water buckets in exchange for trail rides on a school horse called Vandy. While working at the Webster barn, Karen heard of an opportunity to lease a pinto pony called Cherokee.

Children learning to ride often use a school horse owned by a riding stable. To be able to ride more often without making the commitment of buying, sometimes riders lease a horse. Karen had been taking lessons for more than a year when, in 1980, the Brains heard that the Crampton family was living temporarily in France. While they were away, they wanted someone to ride their pony Cherokee to keep her fit. Karen's parents decided that a half-lease on Cherokee would be a perfect Christmas present. The monthly payments were quite reasonable, and the half-lease would give Karen access to the pony three days a week.

Karen and Terri started taking their lessons with Carol Webster. In addition to the girls' weekly riding lesson, Karen rode Cherokee on her own twice a week. Terri also rode several times a week, and with more time in the saddle, both girls steadily improved.

As her confidence and abilities grew, Karen started taking jumping lessons from Lynne Owen, a competitive event rider who boarded two horses of her own at the Webster barn.

Cherokee was a brave and honest pony and she helped Karen conquer her fear of losing control when jumping. In her lessons, Karen learned how to post properly, check that she was on the correct diagonal, and ride comfortably and confidently in the two-point position. She learned how to adjust the length of her reins without dropping them, how to sit at the trot without bouncing around in the saddle, and how to keep her pony straight as they came toward the fences.

On trail rides, Karen often lost track of time, riding Cherokee for hours along the side of the road and on trails winding through the picturesque farmland of the Saanich Peninsula.

Sometimes Karen dragged poles, barrels, jump standards, hay bales, and anything else she could find into the riding ring, where she built big fences. Then she got Cherokee going really fast, pointed her at the jumps, and hung on.

One day, Lynne caught up with Karen in the barn. Lynne asked whether Karen had been responsible for setting up the big jumps. A sinking feeling in Karen's stomach told her she was in trouble. She nodded. Lynne gave her a long, hard look and said, "Don't jump big jumps like that unless you are being supervised in a lesson."

Karen nodded and waited to hear what her punishment would be. Instead, Lynne suggested that maybe Karen was ready to start training to be in a horse show, one where she could enter in some jumping classes. Barely believing her luck, Karen nodded vigorously. A horse show? It seemed as if she had been preparing her whole life to ride in a horse show! She could hardly wait.

Pony Club Spring Show

Though Karen had ridden Vandy in a couple of small walk-trot classes at a local schooling show, riding in a jumping show at the local fairgrounds felt like a huge step forward. Because she had been taking jumping lessons from Lynne for only a short while, they had little time to prepare for Karen's first competitive jumping experience.

Karen was shocked at the long list of tasks she had to complete just so she and Cherokee would look smart for the competition. Karen arranged to borrow a riding jacket from one of her sister's friends. The day before the show, Karen gave Cherokee a bath and then put a stable blanket on her pony to keep her clean overnight. After that, she took all her tack home, where she took her saddle and bridle apart and cleaned and oiled every piece, buffing the leather with a soft cloth until the tack glowed. Though she worked late into the night getting all her show clothes and horse equipment ready, on the morning of May 16, 1981, she was up before dawn to head back to the barn to braid her pony's mane and tail and groom her extra thoroughly.

It was a lot of work to get ready, but Karen loved every minute of it. At last, she hopped aboard Cherokee and rode the short distance down the road to the local fairgrounds.

When the big moment arrived for Karen to ride her pony into the ring, the pair looked fabulous.

In the show ring, Karen's nerves got the better of her as she worried about going off course. Cherokee picked up on her rider's jitters, and they wobbled back and forth as they approached the fences. Karen tried to adjust their speed and improve her steering but she overcorrected and Cherokee got confused. There was too much to think about! The fences

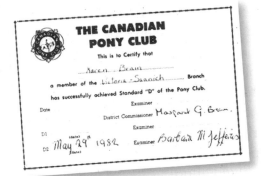

Karen learns a great deal about riding and looking after horses through her involvement with Pony Club. Karen joins Pony Club in 1980, during the time she leases Cherokee, and remains active for many years, eventually helping young Pony Clubbers improve their horsemanship and riding skills. Karen achieves "A" level (the highest level possible) in Canadian Pony Club in 1989.

looked different from the ones at home. These were decorated with flowers, flags, and brightly painted signs belonging to show sponsors. Spectators clapped and cheered, the other riders watched her ride every fence, and, worst of all, a judge noted every mistake.

Karen lost her focus completely and the worst happened: Cherokee ran out, swerving suddenly to avoid jumping. She tossed her head as Karen tried to get her back on course. A hot flush flooded Karen's cheeks. A run-out was a penalty, and too many penalties meant she couldn't win. Somehow Karen managed to hang on and steer around the rest of the course, though her score wasn't very good and she didn't win a ribbon.

Things improved a little as the day went on, and Karen did better in her other classes. She and Cherokee won a fifth-, a fourth-, and two third-place ribbons. Karen's first show left her with mixed feelings. She was relieved that she hadn't fallen off and happy that she had collected some ribbons, but she hadn't won any classes. Things hadn't gone perfectly, and that made Karen determined to do better.

Karen knew that to improve she needed to ride more and take more lessons. Cherokee's owners were coming home soon and that meant Karen needed to find another horse. By this time, Karen and her friend Elizabeth Safranyik were both convinced that they needed to buy horses of their own. The girls plotted and schemed and dreamed about the perfect

down. To keep the delicate mare warm in the winter, she needed to wear two blankets.

It wasn't long before Karen had to admit she had made a terrible mistake. Patty was horrible to ride—hypersensitive, fast, and nervous. Karen was not nearly good enough to ride a powerful, flighty horse like Patty. The combination of an inexperienced rider and a difficult horse could not have been worse. Riding lessons were awful. Patty bolted each time Karen tried to put her leg to the mare's side. In one of her first lessons on Patty, Karen fell off three times! She smashed her tailbone and was in so much pain that for two months she could hardly sit in the saddle. This didn't bother Patty much; she preferred it when Karen stood up in the stirrups. The mare's back was often sore, which contributed to her upright, stiff, and jerky way of moving. Constantly riding in the two-point position did little to improve Karen's riding skills.

What Is Eventing?

Originating as a military test of a horse's obedience, versatility, and ability to travel quickly over rough terrain, eventing involves three distinct phases: dressage, cross-country (endurance), and stadium jumping. Each phase tests a particular set of skills and challenges the horse and rider in a different way. Events take place over one, two, or three days. These competitions are also known as horse trials or combined training events.

Dressage

A reflection of a rider's skill and a horse's obedience, flexibility, and balance, a dressage test includes set combinations of movements performed in a standard-sized arena (usually 20 by 60 metres). A horse and rider in tune with each other will execute even the most challenging manoeuvres smoothly, and only close observation will detect the rider's signals.

Karen and VDL Odette compete at a dressage show at the Saanich Fairgrounds in 2006.

Photo by Nikki Tate

Judges score each movement on a scale of 0 to 10 (with 10 being the highest attainable score). These raw scores are converted into penalty points and added to penalties accumulated in the other phases.

Endurance and Cross-Country

The cross-country jump course is actually one component of the endurance phase of an event. In traditional long-format three-day events, the endurance day includes four sub-phases. Phase A is called roads and tracks. Each horse completes a medium-paced warm-up over an outdoor course (without jumps) as a way to prepare for the steeplechase (Phase B). This warm-up takes place at an active trot over a set distance through fields and along trails. The steeplechase requires the horse to tackle a series of brush fences, which have the top part made of brush that can be jumped through. The solid portion below the brush is what determines the maximum height for the division. An additional 12 inches (30 centimetres) of brush is permitted above that. For example, in a CCI*** event (see sidebar page 59), the solid part is 3 feet 11 inches (1.2 metres), and the addition of the brush part above that makes the overall height of the fence 4 feet 11 inches (1.5 metres). The fences still look quite solid, and some horses will jump the full height of the obstacle until they learn they can brush through the top part of the fence. A certain speed (between 640 metres per minute [mpm] for lower levels and 690 mpm for CCI*** and CCI**** events) is determined ahead of time, and horses are penalized for completing this phase too slowly.

A second roads and tracks (Phase C) has a slower pace (again without obstacles) and is intended to allow the horse to cool down after the steeplechase in preparation for the final and most difficult phase, the cross-country jump course (Phase D). Before starting the cross-country course, a vet checks the horse's temperature, heart rate, and respiration. Horses judged to be unfit or unsound are not allowed to continue.

The cross-country course itself consists of between twelve and forty fences (depending on the level of competition) made of natural materials and located on an outdoor course over natural terrain. Obstacles in this phase might include jumps into and out of

Karen and Merlin clear a fence called the Hay Basket at the Maple Ridge Horse Trials in 1993. Karen and Merlin placed first in the Preliminary division.

27

water, ditches, logs, banks, stone walls, gates, or drops. These fences are solid and do not fall over if a horse knocks or crashes into them. Some obstacles can be tackled several ways. One option might be more difficult but faster while another might be easier but slower.

In recent years, a shorter form of horse trial has eliminated the steeplechase and roads and tracks phases. Even though these competitions are frequently referred to as three-day events, they may take place over as few as one day or as many as four days.

Penalties are incurred on a cross-country course if the rider falls off or a horse refuses a fence, goes off course, or completes the course too slowly (or too quickly at lower levels). Some reasons a rider may be eliminated include jumping an obstacle out of order or in the wrong direction, or missing an obstacle. Riders are not allowed to go out on the course without correct equipment (proper helmet, back protector, and an armband with emergency contact and medical information).

Stadium Jumping

Before horses are allowed to compete in the final phase of the competition (the stadium jumping or show jumping phase), they again must pass a rigorous vet inspection to make sure they have not suffered an injury in the earlier phases. The twelve to twenty obstacles in this phase are set up in a contained ring. Brightly coloured, these fences are designed to be knocked down if a horse bumps them. Each time a rail falls, the horse and rider are assessed four jumping faults. Speed and agility

Karen and Merlin in 1994 in the stadium jumping round at the Whidbey Island three-day event.

are tested in this phase—riders are given faults for each second they take over a pre-established time limit for the course.

Penalty Points and Scoring

Penalty points for each phase are weighted differently. The cross-country course is considered to be the most important component of an event, so penalties accumulated here weigh most heavily against the rider. Penalty points accumulated over all phases are added together, and the horse and rider combination with the fewest penalty points is the winner.

Though lessons on Patty often left Karen bruised and choking back tears, at least she didn't have to travel far to be tortured. At about this time, Lynne Owen moved her eventing horses to Spring Ridge Farm, a small barn within walking distance of Karen's house on the Saanich Peninsula. Karen moved Patty, too.

Despite Patty's challenges, Karen rode her for hours each day. Sometimes she and Elizabeth climbed aboard bareback. They took turns jumping over the ditch at the back of the property and sometimes used logs to build rough and ready cross-country fences. They imagined they were brilliant event riders who rode as well as their coach, Lynne. And in her imagination, Karen became so good that she rode Patty in the Olympics as a member of Canada's national eventing team.

Reality was not so kind. Lessons did little to improve Karen's relationship with Patty. To make matters worse, Elizabeth was a better rider than Karen. Sometimes Karen let her friend ride Patty, and jealousy twisted her insides when Elizabeth managed quite well on the fractious mare.

Horse shows on Patty were a disaster. In flat classes, Patty barged around the ring at top speed with her head in the air, her eyes wide. She hated jumping and galloped around the courses barely under Karen's control. Just when Karen least expected it, Patty hit the brakes and crashed into fences, catapulting Karen out of the saddle and into the dirt.

Patty refuses to jump at a horse show hosted by Spring Ridge Farm on Vancouver Island, 1982.

When the crowds clapped or the announcer's voice crackled over the loudspeaker, Patty went berserk, bolting around the ring in a blind panic, perhaps remembering her days as a racehorse at the track. It wasn't unusual for Karen and her unruly horse to be excused from the ring. These incidents were exciting to watch, but not much fun for Karen.

The successes Karen enjoyed with Patty were few and far between. An attractive horse, Patty won ribbons in halter classes, where Karen led the mare around and showed off her good looks. Karen also did well in some equitation classes (in which the riders are judged on their riding abilities), but the stresses of the larger shows and jumping classes were too much for the high-strung Thoroughbred.

Finally, after nearly a year and a half of frustration, Karen knew that Patty had to go. In 1983, Patty was sold as a broodmare for much less than Karen had paid for her. While it was clear that Karen had bought the wrong horse, it was also very obvious to everyone around her that Karen was completely committed to riding. In some ways, Patty *was* the perfect horse for Karen. If she could survive such a bad experience and still want to ride more than ever, was there any doubt that riding was more than just a passing fancy?

Pumpkin (shown with Karen in 1983) is sensible and quiet, completely different from Patty.

Pumpkin

Pumpkin, a big, pluggy quarter horse that Lynne found for Karen, could not have been more different from Patty.

Unlike Patty, who took off as if she'd been shot out of a cannon each time Karen's legs touched her sides,

Karen and Pumpkin on the cross-country course at Kelvin Creek in Duncan on Vancouver Island in 1983.

Pumpkin required a lot of encouragement just to keep moving. When he did get going, though, he was well-educated, good at what he did, and level-headed.

On his back, Karen relaxed and started to improve. When she entered horse shows, she held her own against the other riders. She and Pumpkin did everything—dressage, jumping, hack classes—and she started to win ribbons consistently. Each time she took home a ribbon, she hung it proudly on the wall of her room alongside her horse posters and photographs.

Karen also experienced a new kind of triumph with Pumpkin. When she first started riding him, he was unfit and didn't look that great. But after Karen started working with him, his condition improved and soon he was sleek and muscled, sporting a glossy coat. At shows, more than one person commented, "I've never seen Pumpkin look so good!"

Karen glowed with each compliment. "I puffed up a bit. I learned that I was creating a whole package, the complete animal. People's praise about how that horse looked outweighed the ribbons. I was learning about horsemanship."

It wasn't long before Karen wanted to try her hand at eventing. But there was so much she didn't know—and didn't think to ask. Lynne suggested that the Pre-Training division one-day event at Kelvin Creek in Duncan would be a suitable first outing for Karen and Pumpkin.

"How will I know where to go?" Karen asked Lynne when they arrived. Would there be arrows to mark the course? Yellow ribbons tied to trees? A short course in a ring was

Can you guess that a horse lover lives here? Karen's room at her Saanichton home in 1984.

one thing. A cross-country course with big jumps hidden in the forest was something else!

"We'll walk the course first," Lynne explained, looking surprised at the question.

Karen felt a little foolish but much relieved, though her relief didn't last long.

Lynne looked like a mother duck with her ducklings trailing behind her as she and her group of students made their way around the course. At each fence, Lynne made suggestions tailored to each horse and rider. She told Karen when to urge Pumpkin on, which line of approach to take to each jump, and which option to choose when an obstacle could be jumped more than one way. Karen could hardly take it all in.

Later, mounted and waiting near the start box, Karen felt a tight knot of anxiety in her stomach. She circled Pumpkin after she received her three-minute warning from the start official and tried to focus on where she needed to go, what she needed to do. The two-minute and one-minute warnings came and went and Karen rode into the start box. There, she held her breath as the final seconds counted down.

Finally, off they went, galloping out onto the course. Karen worked constantly to keep Pumpkin going. The jumps were larger than Karen was used to. When Karen's horse made a big effort to clear a fence, her legs slipped back, which threw her body forward. With her legs out of position she was unbalanced and lacked the strength to apply enough pressure to keep Pumpkin at a canter. To Karen's dismay, he dropped back to a trot, far too slow a pace to get around the course within the time limit and avoid penalty points, let alone build enough momentum to clear the jumps.

Karen managed to get Pumpkin going again, but then something outside the field startled him and he spooked sideways several times during his round. Each time he spooked, Karen had trouble getting him back on a straight line for the next obstacle. Just before one fence, Pumpkin spooked at something in the trees, turned sharply, and ran out at the last moment.

Luckily, Karen didn't fall off, but she hated the feeling of having to fight for every stride. She hung on until the end of the round, and after she cleared the final obstacle she gave her horse a hearty pat on the neck. They hadn't won—not even close—but she and her horse had survived the cross-country course without a major disaster.

Karen wanted more than to survive. She wanted to win. To be truly competitive in eventing circles, Karen knew she needed to do several things. She needed to keep riding, taking lessons, and attending clinics so that she would improve in all areas of her riding. She needed to be physically fitter and stronger. And she needed a better horse.

Pumpkin was wonderful: fun to ride, and good within his limitations. But the hard work sometimes made him lame...and he simply wasn't fast enough.

Karen and Pumpkin (shown in 1983) are a good team, but Karen needs a horse with more potential.

Karen and Alpo

Alpo might have wound up as dog food if he hadn't been spotted by Bridget Flynn, a Vancouver Island riding coach who happened to be at the same auction as the meat-buyers on the day Alpo came up for sale in 1983. Shown here in 1987.

The Little Horse That Could

IT's HARD FOR KAREN TO EXPLAIN, but from the minute she first met Alpine Renegade (better known as Alpo), she felt as if she and the young horse shared a special connection. A six-year-old gelding of uncertain breeding—though most likely at least part Morgan—he had a beautiful face and a round, muscular body.

Lameness plagued Pumpkin, and while he was on a short layoff to see if he would recover well enough for Karen to keep riding, Lynne suggested that Karen try Alpo, whose owner was laid up with a riding injury. At first, Karen wasn't keen to make a permanent switch because she had become very fond of Pumpkin. Lynne changed her approach and asked Karen to help out by riding Alpo to keep him in shape while his owners looked for a buyer.

Karen agreed and rode Alpo in a few lessons. It didn't take long before she lost her heart to the cheeky bay.

Alpo's high energy and spunky personality kept Karen on her toes; she never knew what he might do next. "He was spooky, intense, flighty, snorty, and twitty—a typical delinquent adolescent," Karen says, recalling his early erratic behaviour. Despite these challenges, Karen knew she had to own him. "We were destined to be partners." When a rumour circulated around the barn that a buyer had been found, Karen declared that nobody was going to buy Alpo but her.

Even though she was only thirteen, Karen's frugal ways (she worked hard at her various barn and horse-sitting jobs and saved every penny she received as gifts from relatives) meant that she had enough saved, with the proceeds from Patty's sale, to make an offer on Alpo. Little did Karen know where her partnership with the spunky little horse would take her.

Karen was not the only one in the dark about what lay ahead. Coaches and other riders didn't think Alpo would amount to much. For one thing, he wasn't very big (only 15 hh) and many people wrote him off as being too small—and, therefore, too slow—to make the times required on cross-country courses. Lynne said that Alpo would be able to do everything well enough but would never be a superstar.

Karen worked hard to train both her new horse and herself, and soon the pair began having a lot of fun together and bringing home ribbons. A successful eventing horse must be versatile and consistent in all three phases. The first place where Karen's hard work began to pay off was in the dressage ring. Always confident in her flatwork, Karen enjoyed the time she spent schooling in the ring. But early in their partnership, Alpo was hard to ride in the jumping competitions. He was insecure as he approached the fences, and it was sometimes hard for Karen to keep him going

stronger finishes at ever bigger competitions. More and more ribbons, including many firsts, took their places on Karen's walls. Each time someone said that Alpo had reached his limit, Karen asked for more, and he responded.

In 1985, at a Pony Club rally in Maple Ridge, Karen and Alpo won their first Pre-Training event. Lynne was absolutely thrilled and Karen was excited and horrified at the same time. Alpo had been spooky and balked at many of the jumps on the cross-country course. Every step was a fight, and though he somehow made it around the course, during her round Karen could think only of the plans Lynne had for her at a show two weeks away. There, Karen and Alpo were to move up a division, but after Alpo's sluggish reaction on the cross-country course, Karen could not imagine surviving the ordeal! As they would do so many times in their career together, they rose to the challenge and managed to compete successfully at the higher level.

Travel to shows was usually a lot of fun but could be fraught with unforeseen accidents. One of the most frightening incidents in Karen's early show career didn't happen on a course but just minutes from her house, in the parking lot of the Swartz Bay ferry terminal. Karen and another young event rider were in the truck with a driver, waiting to drive onto the ferry's car deck. Behind them, their horses Alpo and Luke were in a horse trailer. When they pulled forward, another car shot in front of them, racing for the ferry. The driver of the truck slammed on the brakes to avoid hitting the other vehicle. Luke's feet slipped out from under him, and the horse fell in the confined space of the trailer.

Alarmed by the loud banging, the girls jumped out of the truck and opened the small side doors of the trailer to see what had happened. Luke half hung, half sprawled inside, and when they opened the safety door, one of his forelegs shot out.

Karen's friend panicked, convinced that her horse was going to die. Onlookers ran to help, and it took several of them to undo Luke's lead rope and force his leg back inside the trailer. Unable to get to his feet, Luke twisted sideways and slipped in the other direction. All four legs now extended beneath the partition and right under Alpo.

"We have to get my horse out of there!" Karen was adamant.

With the ramp down, she encouraged Alpo to back out of the trailer. As if he understood how careful he had to be, Alpo gingerly picked up each foot and placed it so he would not step on the fallen horse's legs. More people rushed to help. Alpo, despite the shouts and bangs from the trailer, stood quietly and waited. With a huge effort, Luke was hauled to his feet. Shaky but none the worse for wear, he was backed out. After being thoroughly checked over, both horses were loaded back into the trailer and Karen and her friend went on to compete in the event on the mainland as they had planned.

Other traumas were less obvious to outside observers. During the recession of the 1980s, many families suffered terrible financial hardship when interest rates were high and real estate deals crumbled. The Brain family was no exception. Though they went through some difficult financial times, Karen's parents steadfastly refused to let Karen sacrifice her

riding or consider giving Alpo up. Even though her parents did their best to shield their daughters, Karen was well aware that money was not easy to come by. During the worst

In 1985, Karen builds a rough and ready jump in her back yard. Don't try this at home!

period, she noticed her father's uncharacteristic seriousness and missed his joking around and easy laughter. She awoke from one nightmare weeping, irrationally convinced that her father was going to start robbing banks to help pay the family bills.

Creativity, determination, and mutual loving support saw the family through even the roughest patches. "You don't need the fanciest show clothes," Karen says. "What you need is a will to succeed and a desire to achieve. Even if I had wealthy parents, without the moral support I have always received I couldn't have made it."

Banquets and Podiums: The Thrill of Success

In 1986, when she was sixteen, Karen won a gigantic high-point ribbon for being the junior British Columbia rider to accumulate the most points at approved shows during the previous show season. The award was a great excuse for Karen and some of her riding friends to attend the annual British Columbia Combined Training Association (now Horse Trials B.C.) awards banquet held in Vancouver.

1986: Karen with her high-point ribbon awarded by the B.C. Combined Training Association.

The following year Karen set her sights on the Western Canada Summer Games. She and Alpo easily qualified for the Preliminary-level three-day event held in Regina. Unlike most of her earlier outings, where she had competed as an individual, this time Karen rode as part of a team representing her home province of British Columbia. Karen always put pressure on herself to ride well whenever she competed, but riding for a team added another layer of stress. She was the youngest member of the B.C. team, but she was determined to do well. "Whatever happened, I didn't want to be the dropped score," she says, referring to the way the team scores are calculated by eliminating the lowest result.

Despite an uncharacteristic stop by Alpo on the cross-country course, the B.C. team was in contention for a medal as they headed into the final day of competition. Karen's round in the stadium jumping was strong and confident, and she needn't have worried about having her score dropped. When all the scores were tallied, her teammate Dale Irwin won the individual gold medal and Karen came in fifth overall, garnering the second-highest score for the B.C. team. The team's results were good enough that she also received a team gold medal to add to her collection of prizes. As she had wanted more than anything, she had contributed to her team's final placing. She and Alpo returned home champions.

At every opportunity, Karen attended clinics. Top equestrians like England's Captain Mark Phillips travel widely to teach up-and-coming riders around the world. In 1972, Captain Phillips and the rest of his country's team had won Olympic gold for the three-day event. When he offered a clinic in Vancouver in 1987, Karen signed up and loved the time she was able to spend working with one of her riding idols.

That same year, Karen competed in many, many events, some as far away as California. Each outing taught her something new, and it wasn't long before

The B.C. eventing team collects gold medals at the Western Canada Summer Games in Regina in 1987. Dale Irwin (front) is also the individual gold medalist.

41

Captain Mark Phillips adjusts Karen's lower leg position, 1987.

both she and her little horse, Alpo, were seasoned competitors.

Karen's family sometimes combined travel to events and clinics with vacations, and they kept expenses down by camping on-site, preparing meals in the camper, and pooling resources with other families by sharing gas costs and trailer space.

"Lynne [Owen] was incredibly generous in that way," Karen says. "She never charged coaching fees and she would split the ferry costs with us." Karen covered more and more of her own expenses by increasing the number of hours she worked each week. While still a teenager, she worked toward getting her Level 1 coaching certification and, through Pony Club, began to teach younger students who were just learning to ride.

Unlike many of Karen's classmates, who enjoyed parties, dances, and shopping expeditions, horse show banquets and award ceremonies were the only social outings Karen had time for. Karen's last year of high school was one long blur of lessons, clinics, and ever bigger horse shows. Her training and competition schedule was so intense that she had to get special permission to write some of her final exams early. Rituals like shopping for a graduation gown fell by the wayside, and finding a date for the grad dance was just not a priority. When Karen's mother pushed her to take a couple of hours during an event near Portland, Oregon, to go dress shopping, Karen could only say, "Mom! I just don't care about the dance!" What Karen did care about was getting to the Olympics. Her graduation write-up in her yearbook reads, "[In] five years she plans to be polishing an Olympic Gold Medal."

Though Karen learned a lot competing on the west coast of Canada and the United States, in 1988 she decided to move to Ontario, where she could take advantage of larger events held in eastern Canada and the U.S.

Leaving Home

In 1988, at the age of eighteen, Karen secured a working student position with Nick Holmes-Smith, one of Canada's best event riders. Over the years, Karen had attended clinics taught by Holmes-Smith, and Lynne, who had grown up eventing with Holmes-Smith in B.C., put in a good word for her young protégée.

Karen was ready to leave home and do her own thing and didn't have any reservations about moving across the country to pursue her riding. Once she got there, though, she initially found it hard to make friends. Many of the other riders were much older, and they liked to not only work hard, but play hard. One of them suggested that Karen was just too young to leave home, a notion Karen scoffed at. "I was never much of a partier," Karen says, "but that didn't mean I was immature." It wasn't until she found a few like-minded buddies to hang around with that she really started enjoying her new community in Ontario. "I had to decide whether I would change who I was and start partying like the others just to fit in. I knew who I was and I wasn't going to do that."

Though it took a little time to get her social life sorted out, she quickly settled into the daily routine demanded of a working student, first at Holmes-Smith's farm and then, after a couple of months, at another Ontario barn. During that summer, Holmes-Smith and the other members of Canada's national eventing team were busy preparing to ride in the 1988 Olympic Games. Being around these top-level riders made Karen realize just what was involved in getting herself and her horse ready for international competition.

Karen and Alpo ready to tackle the cross-country course at the Gatwick Horse Trials in England, April 1989.

Stroud, Gloucestershire. The estate features stables, riding rings, and a cross-country course where riders from all over the world compete at huge international events.

Each day the girls completed stable chores, had riding lessons and clinics—taught by top-level riders like Captain Mark Phillips, Mark Todd (the New Zealand eventer voted Rider of the 20th Century), and William Micklem (the Irish Young Riders event coach at Gleneagles)—and attended lectures in fitness and nutrition.

Later that spring, after the students had moved to Gatcombe Park in England, the young riders also competed in horse shows and events. Karen's parents flew to England to watch her compete at large shows like the Gatwick Horse Trials in April.

Though Karen was thrilled about being challenged by big courses and huge jumps, competing over courses like those she encountered in England had hazardous moments. At the first of Karen's events in England, she made an error riding toward a big ditch jump. Alpo's size meant he often banked the larger cross-country fences, using his back feet to push off them as he jumped across (banking can also refer to a horse touching down on top of an obstacle with all four feet, which is acceptable as long as the horse gets across). This jump was a large triple-bar oxer made of three ascending logs suspended over a wide, deep, natural ditch. Alpo didn't have quite enough momentum to clear the ditch cleanly, so he tried to push off the lowest (first) log with his back legs while still in mid-air. His hind hooves slipped backward and his back legs failed to clear the fence, slipping instead between the two lower logs. His forelegs hung down between the two higher logs, and his belly rested on the middle log. Karen found herself sitting on her horse in perfect riding position, unable to do a thing to help him. Gingerly, she climbed off, horrified at the situation in which her poor horse now found himself.

Riders coming behind had to be stopped and the cross-country phase delayed until heavy equipment could be brought in to dismantle the fence and free the suspended horse. First the crew took down the highest log. This meant Alpo had no support under his chest or neck, and while they worked frantically to free his back legs, he hung, head down, into the ditch. The ditch was so deep, his nose didn't reach the ground! (To help prevent such accidents, current eventing rules do not allow ditches this deep.)

Up until the ditch incident, Alpo had never had an injury or an accident. He was a small horse with a huge heart, a horse who always tried to do whatever Karen asked. The accident really knocked the stuffing out of him, and it took months before he was back in top form and willing to tackle the big obstacles asked of him at serious events. It didn't help that Karen found it hard to ask him to do the jumps that now made him uneasy. She, too, had lost a little of her nerve, and it took time to get it back.

Captain Mark Phillips did his best to help the two recover. Sometimes he took Karen and Alpo out to school on different cross-country courses. Though the Captain was generous with his time and encouragement, he was also tough and unforgiving if he thought Karen was doing something foolish with her horse. He didn't try to save her feelings when, after Karen made a mistake, he said, "You are going to ruin your horse if you ever do that again! He'll never get his confidence back if you ride him like that!"

Karen was upset after these scoldings, but never because of what the Captain was telling her. She was upset because she was making mistakes. Each time she was told off she became more determined to improve her riding. "I never questioned the Captain's judgment—I knew he was completely right." Karen was humbled but knew how important it was to fix the problem. "I couldn't afford to screw up—the consequences were too great! I wanted the Captain to think highly of me. I needed to show him that I could do what he was asking."

Despite Karen's extra practice with the Captain, ditch jumps continued to prove troublesome. At the last horse trial Karen competed in during her stay in Great Britain, she and Alpo enjoyed a great round in the cross-country phase—until they galloped toward the twenty-first fence. It was a ditch with a fence, and, sure enough, Alpo refused three times and they were eliminated. The Captain stood and watched, and Karen could do nothing to get her horse over the fence.

Diplomatically, the Captain suggested that if Karen wanted to continue in the sport of eventing, she might have to consider finding another horse, one that was a little bigger and better able to handle the demands of upper level competition.

Darlene Brain stands in front of the Badminton jump known as Luckington Lane, May 1989. Photo by Bill Brain

For exposure to the kinds of obstacles they might someday face, the young riders attended the Whitbread Championships at Badminton in May. There, the Captain walked the CCI**** course with his students.

When the group came to a huge natural log suspended over a big ditch, Karen looked up at the massive fence. "And that," the Captain said with his characteristic dry sense of humour, "is about as far as you would get, Karen. You and your little horse would have to go under this one."

While Karen's parents were proud, they were also horrified to see the size of some of the obstacles their daughter might have to tackle if she continued with her chosen sport.

Heartbreak

After three months of training and competition in England, Karen and Alpo flew back to Canada and returned to work at another barn in Ontario. Karen continued to compete with Alpo but was increasingly worried about how far he would be able to go. They did well at the Bromont three-day event in Quebec, a Preliminary competition, but were penalized for not being fast enough. Unbeknownst to Karen, team officials had rated Alpo as an Intermediate-graded horse, which meant he needed to complete the course faster than horses with lower ratings in order to avoid penalties. The time faults cost them the win. But even if she had known about the rating change, Karen might not have been able to push her horse any harder. "I loved Alpo too much to *have* to use the whip to keep encouraging him to make the speed during the gallops."

Not quite sure how to proceed, Karen phoned the national team office and asked, "How do I get long-listed for the Canadian team?"

The team representative explained that, first and foremost, Karen needed a horse that had the potential to make the short-listed team. She wondered aloud whether Karen's "little horse" was good enough to win at the highest levels. Though Karen already knew the answer, she asked, "What should I do?"

"Sell your horse and get a new one."

"Do you know of anything suitable?"

The team spokesperson thought she might know of a team-level horse for lease, so Karen, her heart breaking, put the word out that Alpo was for sale. Not long after, she took part in a clinic with trainer Jack Le Goff, an internationally renowned rider, Olympic-level judge, and former coach of the United States eventing team. Le Goff loved Alpo and, through one of his contacts, arranged for a woman from California to fly out and try him. Alpo passed the vet examination with flying colours and the sale was quickly completed. Karen's partner of the last seven years—seven years during which they'd both matured into polished eventers—now belonged to someone else.

The next few weeks were agony for Karen, who continued to ride Alpo to keep him in top condition for his new owner. When the day came to load him into the trailer to be shipped to California, she was devastated. She had prepared his feed and written out clear instructions for the shippers and for his new owner. When she saw him peek out the trailer window, she thought her heart would break. She knew that at each stop he would be looking for her, and for the first time in years she would not be there. The sense of betrayal was horrendous, and after the truck pulled away, Karen slumped on her tack box. Furious with herself for having sold her best friend, she beat her dressage whip against the top of the tack box and collapsed into tears.

While some at the barn were sympathetic to her grief and offered her support, others were less understanding. One man went so far as to call her a stupid girl whose horse would now wind up on the American Olympic eventing team.

Karen felt so alone and miserable that she struggled to remember what she was doing in Ontario so far from home. She began to second-guess herself. Why had she sold her horse? How could she go on without him?

Karen gives Alpo a kiss in Santa Rosa, California, in October 1990 during a visit she made to see her horse in his new home.

3

Merlin's Magic

Karen clears a narrow fence in the stadium jumping phase of the Maple Ridge Horse Trials in 1993.

No Going Back

WITH EIGHTEEN THOUSAND DOLLARS in her pocket, Karen called the national team office again and relayed the news that she had sold Alpo. The reaction was not what she expected. The woman seemed to forget what she had told Karen during the earlier conversation. She sounded shocked that Karen had sold "that stunning little horse?" The only horse she knew of that might be suitable as a replacement was a five-year-old on the market for twenty-five thousand dollars. The horse she had initially thought might be available for lease had been placed elsewhere.

Karen felt ill. *Oh, no…what have I done?* she despaired.

Thousands of kilometres away from home, her beloved Alpo sold, Karen slid into a depression. She looked at a number of horses but none was suitable. They were all either too young, too expensive, or unsound. Bitter and unhappy, she raged against everyone who had ever suggested that she might need to sell Alpo and find another horse. But most of all, she was furious with herself. She wanted Alpo back. Or, at the very least, she wished she had held out for more money so she could buy the right horse.

As it was, Karen had no horse to ride and desperately missed her friends and family back in B.C. Despondent and convinced she had made a career-ending mistake, Karen took the proceeds from the sale of Alpo and headed for the refuge of home. After six months of feeling miserable there, she set off with a backpack to see the world. She travelled to New Zealand, Australia, England, Sweden, and Norway, restless and without a clear sense of where she was going. Weeping, she called home from a pay phone in New Zealand. "I just want Alpo back," she wailed. Back on Vancouver Island, listening to the heartbreak in her daughter's voice, Karen's mother felt absolutely helpless.

Travel can sometimes help to make a break with the past and set the traveller on a new path. In New Zealand, Karen met a British girl at a backpackers' hostel and they decided to check out a local trail-riding establishment. The girls enjoyed a good gallop, and after their ride they shared a meal and their stories. The parallels were striking. Both girls had owned and adored dark brown geldings during their teen years, and both had accomplished a great deal on the show circuit because of their equine partners.

After her parents sold her pony when she got too old to ride him in competition (in England, riders over the age of sixteen have to move up from ponies to larger horses), the other girl had plunged into a deep depression. She stopped eating and became so ill with anorexia she wound up in the hospital.

As Karen listened, she realized that her newfound friend was worse off than she was. Karen had survived her loss without becoming ill. *I'm not alone*, she thought. *You truly understand!*

After dinner, Karen called her mother. As she related the other girl's story, she had the sensation of seeing millions of doves flying away from somewhere within her. "This," she understood, "is letting go." As Karen reflected on the lifting of grief, she figured out that she had been afraid to let go, afraid that she wouldn't feel love for Alpo anymore. Feeling the agonizing, internalized pain of missing her horse and wishing to get him back was like proof that she still adored him. When Karen realized she could still love him with all her heart without feeling bad, she was able to release her grief and move forward.

Karen continued with her travels and, after eight months, returned to Vancouver Island refreshed and healed.

Paddy and Merlin

When Lynne Owen heard that Karen was coming home, she immediately came up with a plan. A student had broken his leg, and while it mended he needed someone to ride his horse, Paddy.

Karen, now twenty-two years old, was perfect for the job. She began to ride again and also started doing barn work for Bo Mearns, a former Olympic show jumper and owner of Hunt Valley, a large barn near Victoria. Karen began to teach again but still felt incomplete without a horse partner on whom she could focus her attention.

A couple of times while Karen was working she noticed a black horse heading for a riding lesson. There was something about the horse that intrigued her, but she had no reason to think that the slightly built Thoroughbred ex-racehorse was for sale or, if he was, that he would be within her price range. Karen was making payments on a used pickup truck and had only a few thousand dollars left after her travels. She knew it would never be enough to buy a competition-ready horse.

Chatting with Bo one day, Karen said that she needed to find a horse to train and compete with. Bo thought she might know of one. An image of the black horse popped into Karen's mind, but she pushed it away, saying to herself, "Don't get your hopes up. It probably isn't him."

At the appointed time to view the potential mount, Karen came around the corner and into the riding ring and there he was, the slender black horse. Without even sitting on him, Karen knew that she had to own Merlin. She didn't know *how* she knew, but the feeling was so strong that it blocked out all the negative remarks she would soon hear from other people.

Merlin's owner admitted she had tried to sell the seven-year-old gelding before but nobody wanted to buy him because he was so crazy. He was so sensitive he had to wear earplugs to be ridden. He reacted to every little sound. A pole rolling or sand hitting a panel sent him scooting forward or leaping sideways, bug-eyed and snorting. But in spite of these ominous warning signs, Karen was drawn to the horse in the same powerful way she had first been attracted to Alpo. She counted her pennies, made an offer, and before she knew it, she was once again hard at work training a difficult horse. Karen gave the 15.3 hh Thoroughbred a new show name: Double Take.

Merlin wasn't just hard to ride, he was also difficult to handle on the ground. He exhibited a lot of aggressive, stud-like behaviour. His previous

Paddy provides the motivation Karen needs to get back in the saddle. Vancouver Island, 1992.

owner had been so afraid of him that she wouldn't go into his paddock or stall without a pitchfork, ready to fend off an attack. Karen was worried that he would hurt someone, and she wouldn't let anyone inexperienced get near him. Her intuition on this front was well-founded. Many years later, Karen learned that during his time at the racetrack, Merlin had once kicked a trainer, breaking the man's leg. Beaten as a youngster, Merlin had learned to fight back and twice cornered Karen in an effort to intimidate. His strategy worked only until Karen figured out how to deal with his dangerous attitude. "I had to learn just how much I could discipline him without crossing the line that would trigger an aggressive reaction." Just being nice to him didn't work. "He needed definite boundaries and once he knew his limits, he was better to deal with."

Under saddle, Merlin was easily distracted, his busy brain noticing absolutely everything. During a jumping lesson at Bo's, if someone came into the ring, Merlin's attention shifted from Karen to the visitor, even if he was halfway down a line of jumps. Yet he was so athletic and nimble that he still managed to get over the jumps without touching a rail.

Merlin's reputation preceded him into the show ring. At a schooling show at Bo's, another rider asked Karen, "Are you riding Merlin for his owner?"

"No. I just bought him," Karen replied.

The other rider looked taken aback. "Well," she said finally, "he is cute!"

Karen said nothing, but inside she bristled. Each negative comment just made her more determined. "One day," she vowed, "people will look at this horse and regret what they said about him."

But success did not come quickly or easily.

For the first two years, Karen and her new horse struggled in a love-hate relationship as both of them tried to get, and keep, the upper hand (or hoof). The more Merlin rebelled, the more determined Karen became to make him understand his job. She felt an intuitive connection with the horse who in some ways mirrored her own tough, stubborn, quirky personality. At times she couldn't stand him. At other times she could not believe she had found another horse with whom she shared such a profound bond.

Karen and Merlin in Kelowna, 1992.

Persistence Pays Off

From the beginning, Merlin showed signs of brilliance, though setbacks were frequent. At an event in 1992, Karen and Merlin came in first. Karen trained hard, insisting that Merlin be obedient and accept the partnership she offered.

In 1992, after doing well at Pre-Training and Training events, Karen moved up to the Preliminary division, and in 1993, Double Take won the Area VII Preliminary Championships in Oregon and the Preliminary Championships in Maple Ridge. Merlin soared through these, strong and bold to the fences. Thinking about her nutty horse with his prickly personality, Karen felt a strong rush of affection. When she stopped comparing him to "the perfect horse" (Alpo) and accepted who Merlin was, the tension between them lessened and all his idiosyncrasies became endearing traits to appreciate.

Karen shows off her trophy and ribbon after winning the Preliminary division at Freeman Farms in Oregon, 1993.

In 1994 and 1995, new difficulties arose. Merlin didn't like water jumps. Lynne suggested that Karen sell Merlin and move on to an easier horse. Karen wanted to persevere. She insisted that, with more work, Merlin had what it took to make it to the top. Karen believed that he had Olympic potential and that together they could qualify for the national team.

Karen dug in her heels and refused to switch to another horse. For a while, things were tense between Karen and her long-time coach. Karen continued training with Bo Mearns (who worked with her on show jumping technique) and also began to get help from Nick Holmes-Smith (who had relocated to British Columbia) to improve her performance on the cross-country course. Their number one challenge was to help Merlin overcome his water jump problems.

Holmes-Smith had established a cross-country course at Chase Creek, not far from Kamloops in the interior of B.C. His forte had always been cross-country, and Karen attended several clinics at his new training facility. There, she had the luxury of being able to focus on riding in and out of the huge water jump complex. Holmes-Smith had an aggressive riding and coaching style and he taught Karen how to insist that Merlin jump into, through, and out of the water without hesitation.

Karen asked the coach whether he felt Merlin had enough potential or whether she should consider selling him and trying to find an easier horse. Holmes-Smith liked the way Karen and Merlin showed consistent and steady improvement and felt she should probably hang on to the horse. He advised Karen to give herself a time frame, to decide how long she was willing to work with Merlin in order to bring him up to a certain standard. Then she was to assess their progress

Double Take, better known as Merlin, in 1993.

International Event Rating

International events fall under the jurisdiction of the FEI (Fédération Equestre Internationale), known in English as the International Federation for Equestrian Sports.

CCI (Concours Complet International, or International Complete Contest) is a long-format (three-day) event for international competitors.

CIC (Concours International Combiné, or International Combined Contest) is a short-format event for international competitors that may be run over one, two, or three days.

CCIO (Concours Complet International Officiel, or Official International Complete Contest) is an international team competition and is the designation given to the Olympics, the Pan-Am Games, and the World Equestrian Games (also referred to as the World Championships).

The difficulty of an International event is indicated by the number of stars following the event designation. A CCI* is a long-format event for horses just starting out in international competition. A four-star event presents the highest level of difficulty. There are only a handful of these international four-star competitions including those held each year at Badminton, England, and Kentucky, U.S.A. The Olympics and the World Championships are both four-star competitions. Riders able to compete at this level are considered to be among the best in the world.

In terms of difficulty, one-, two-, and three-star competitions are similar, respectively, to the Preliminary, Intermediate, and Advanced levels of Canadian and American competitions.

In a successful show at Spruce Meadows in Calgary, Alberta, in 1995, Karen and Merlin take home third- and fourth-place ribbons in the 4' 6" Jumper Division.

and decide whether or not to sell. "He empowered me to make my own decisions, even if they were going to be hard."

Karen redoubled her efforts, and in the fall of 1995, she and Merlin competed at an event at Chase Creek. At the same event the year before, Merlin had had two stops at the water jump. In 1995, they finished second. After a stunning cross-country round, both Karen and her mother were emotional. Through tears Darlene said, "Your little horse did it!"

By the spring of 1996, Merlin was really jumping well. But he injured a splint bone on the inside of his hind leg with an unfortunate bang on a jump at a July event at Sun Valley, Idaho. Because of the time off he needed to recover, eventing plans for that fall had to be scratched.

Karen knew that to make it at top levels, she would need a second horse. More depth in her horses would mean she could train hard without overextending one horse and, should an injury occur, could still compete on her second mount. While Merlin was recovering from his injury, she decided to buy a little mare called Mazerati, Matzi for short. Money, though, was a problem.

Karen's sister, Terri, and Terri's husband, Rob Gold, wanted to help. "We don't want you to be offended," Terri said, "but would you mind if we all bought Matzi together?" Her idea was to resell Matzi for a profit after Karen had trained her. They all took the plunge, Terri and Rob providing the money and Karen the expertise and willingness to work with the young mare.

Karen continued to work at Hunt Valley, increasing her roster of students (by this time she had earned her Level 2 coaching certification). She taught clinics, ran Pony Club camps, and helped others train their horses. Even so, there never seemed to be quite enough money, and when she needed to purchase a horse trailer, her parents helped her buy a used one.

By the fall of 1996, Karen was ready to take a run at making the national team. Merlin had shown his potential and she was determined that Peter Gray, the team coach, also recognize what a great horse Merlin could be.

Gray watched Karen ride both her horses at a clinic but said that while Karen's talents were obvious, and the horses performed well in stadium jumping and dressage, he did not believe that Merlin was yet ready for Advanced-level competition in cross-country. Karen wasn't discouraged. Merlin was still not fully fit and Matzi was only at Training level and lacked experience. Besides, the mare wasn't necessarily supposed to take Karen to the top—she had been bought as a resale project.

When Peter Gray suggested that Karen stay in British Columbia for another year, preparing for stiffer competition in eastern Canada and in the United States, Karen shook her head. She believed that she had the talent to move on—that she and Merlin needed to go to Florida, train there, and compete at a challenging event like the Rolex Kentucky CCI*** event the following spring. She wasn't satisfied anymore with regional competitions; she wanted to move on to bigger challenges.

Lynne advised Karen to think carefully before making a decision to move. She asked Karen whether she fully understood what level of commitment was needed if she

Karen is happy to be competing at the Rolex Kentucky CCI*** in 1997. The pair finished twenty-seventh, in the top third of the field.

hoped to compete in the elite circles of the world's best riders. Lynne warned Karen that if she was going to pursue a riding career at that level, she would have to move away and give up her most important relationships,including her fiancé, Darren. Was she prepared to sacrifice everything?

Karen was resolute. She asked Peter Gray if he knew of a good farm in Florida where she could stay and train with her horses while she prepared for Kentucky. He did. The die was cast.

Karen and Matzi at the Rolex Kentucky Three-Day Event in 1999.

4

Hitting the Big Time

Karen and Merlin gallop cross-country at the World Equestrian Games in Rome, 1998.

Off to Florida

Vancouver island's worst snowstorm in a hundred years delayed Karen's planned departure at the end of December 1996, but she and her horses finally hit the road early in January 1997. Travelling with her friend Laura Hatt, Karen made the long trip to a farm near Ocala, Florida, in the middle of winter, hauling her horses with her old truck and horse trailer. For the next several years she split her time between the U.S. and Ontario.

When Karen headed south, she didn't just leave behind a bit of bad weather. She had been dating Darren Law for several years, and at Christmas 1994 the couple had become

engaged. When she left her fiancé, it was with the understanding she would be returning after the Rolex event in April. Karen was excited to be heading off to pursue her dreams; it was much harder for Darren to be left behind.

Once in Florida, Karen wasted no time. She worked hard to get Merlin fit and Matzi ready to compete. Early in 1997 she rode Matzi and Merlin in horse trials at Morven Park (Leesburg, Virginia) and Southern Pines in North Carolina. Karen felt she had found her place in the world. She was comfortable with the fierce competition and identified with the intense, driven personalities of those determined to make it to the top. And Merlin was right there with her.

In February, Merlin and Karen competed in an Intermediate event at Pine Top Farm in Thomson, Georgia, their first horse trial after the injury in Idaho eighteen months earlier. Two weeks later they completed their first ever Advanced-level horse trial. The pair jumped clean in the cross-country, placed fifth overall, and earned the first of four scores needed to qualify for the Kentucky CCI*** to be held in April.

Karen took part in a training camp for potential Canadian national team members, and in a meeting with the coach and team psychologist she spoke right up.

"I want to go to Kentucky, jump around clean on the cross-country, and finish in the top third so I can get short-listed [for the Canadian national team]. Then I'd be able to ride at the European Championships in the fall of 1997, and that would qualify me for the World Equestrian Games in Rome in 1998, the Pan-Am Games in 1999, and the Olympics in 2000."

Yes, she was a relative rookie, but Karen thought her plan was solid. Then she listened to the other riders stating such modest goals as "achieve a better dressage score" or "have a clean stadium round," and she slumped lower and lower in her chair. Didn't anyone else want to get to the Olympics? She knew that couldn't be true, yet nobody else was saying so out loud.

Peter Gray commented that though Karen's plan was ambitious, he had hoped to hear more of the other riders share similar intentions and their strategies for attaining their goals. The sports psychologist, however, worried that by setting such lofty goals, Karen was setting herself up for failure. Karen stiffened in her seat but held her tongue. She might have big dreams, but she was still realistic. Her goal was to compete in Kentucky and finish in the top third, but if she rode well and finished just out of the top group, she would still be satisfied. And it wouldn't stop her from trying to do better in the next event.

Having laid out her strategy, Karen buckled down to her training regime with Merlin. In April 1997, Karen, Merlin, and Matzi travelled from Florida to Kentucky to compete at the Rolex Kentucky Three-Day Event held each year at the Kentucky Horse Park near Lexington. Despite a technical stop (choosing to take one of the options at a big jump, Karen unintentionally crossed her tracks at the approach and was penalized as a result), Karen and Merlin still did well. She achieved her goal of jumping all the fences cleanly at the Rolex event and finished in the top third.

Karen's consistent results made it impossible to dismiss the idealistic upstart, and team officials took note. Team membership still wasn't assured, though, as other, more experienced riders were also vying for spots and competing well.

Calling home to tell Darren of her results and to let him know she had added some additional competitions to her schedule later in the year, Karen faced the difficult situation that Lynne had predicted months earlier.

"You're not coming home, are you?" Darren asked.

Karen confirmed his fears. Darren let her know he could no longer be part of their long-distance relationship.

While heartbreaking on one hand, it seemed to Karen almost inevitable that their relationship would come to an end. "I think it's possible to have your cake and eat it too," she says, "but just not at the same time."

Now considered to be a long-listed team member (though certainly in contention, Karen had not yet been short-listed for the national team), Karen embarked on an intense period of travel and competition with Merlin and Matzi. For the next year, she and her horses spent time training and competing in Florida, Ontario, and Virginia. The training regime was taxing, but Karen's overwhelming feeling was that she was finally where she belonged. She formed friendships in the eventing world and enjoyed the easy camaraderie she found with her peers. She no longer felt that she stuck out like a sore thumb—her ambition, tenacity, and aggressive riding style were mirrored in the other riders against whom she competed and with whom she became friends.

"It felt like I had come home—I wasn't at all intimidated or uncomfortable," Karen says. "I was where I was meant to be, with people who understood me."

Matzi campaigned well in 1997 and 1998, winning several events in Ontario and placing well in increasingly higher divisions at events in Florida, North Carolina, Virginia, Maryland, and Texas.

In October 1997, Karen finished twelfth with Merlin at the Fair Hill ccɪ*** in Maryland (the top placing for a Canadian), adding to her reputation as a tough competitor. Because she'd finished in the top third in two CCI*** events, Karen had now qualified to compete at the World Championships in Rome. Whether or not Canada would name her to the team was another matter.

Nearly a year later, in early September 1998, Karen won the Canadian National Championships on Merlin, and it was only after this win that Peter Gray gave her the nod. She had secured one of the coveted berths on the national team and would compete for Canada at the World Equestrian Games in Rome in October 1998. The four-star event was an Olympic qualifier, and Karen set her sights on a successful finish in Rome and a spot on the team that would compete in Sydney, Australia, in 2000. Karen and Merlin were at the top of their game and Karen was thrilled.

Making the team also meant the assurance of some financial support from the federal government to help cover her training expenses. Caring for and competing with two horses was very expensive, though, so Karen continued to teach, worked with young horses for other riders, and occasionally earned a commission when she helped broker a sale. She kept her living expenses down by living in her camper and doing barn work to offset her horse board. Being a carded athlete meant that it was a little easier to solicit sponsorship from private sources, and small amounts of money dribbled

*Karen and Merlin clear the pumpkin jump at the Fair Hill CCI*** in Maryland in 1997. The top Canadians, the pair finished twelfth overall.*

in from individuals who had known Karen throughout her riding career.

Though somehow she always managed to provide top-notch care for her horses, financial worries were never far from her mind. The fiscal stress did not deter Karen from focusing her full attention on the task at hand: doing well at the World Equestrian Games. She made it clear to team coach Peter Gray that she had no interest in travelling to Europe if she wasn't going to contribute to the team. If she or her horse wasn't ready, she wouldn't go.

"Even though I was so excited about going to the Worlds," Karen says, "I never lost sight of the fact that I had to be realistic, that I had to stay in control of the decisions I was making."

Karen's final weeks of training stayed on track, her horse

was fit and ready to go, and when she boarded the plane that would take her to Europe and the World Equestrian Games, Karen was jubilant.

Matzi and Karen take a tumble at the water jump at the Camino Real CCI** in Texas, 1998. What does a rider do after a fall like that? Hop back on and finish the course—soaking wet!
Photos courtesy Shannon Brinkman

World Equestrian Games, Rome

Unlike Karen, Merlin was not happy during the long flight to Europe. By the time the group arrived in Zurich and loaded the horse van destined for Italy, he was lethargic and refusing to drink. Upon arrival at the Italian border, Karen knew Merlin was in trouble. She held his head in her arms and demanded a vet, refusing to continue the trip until her horse received treatment. She used a syringe to squirt water into his mouth until the vet arrived to give him intravenous fluids. Merlin had contracted shipping fever, a bacterial infection that affects about 10 percent of horses in transport.

The only other three-day event rider to compete for Canada in 1998 was Stuart Black on his horse Market Venture. The two riders, their horses, and the support team arrived in Rome ten days before the competition, and Merlin was in no shape to do much of anything. Karen nursed her partner, consulting daily with Peter Gray and the team vet, Dr. Alan Young, who continued to monitor Merlin's condition. Slowly, the results of the blood tests started to improve. But the clock was ticking. While Stuart and Market Venture worked on final preparations for the event, Karen could only

KAREN PREPARES
FOR R & Tracks,
STEEPLECHASE &
CROSS-COUNTRY.

WRITES TIMES &
SPEEDS ON ARM,
WEARS TWO WATCHES
FOR DIFFERENT
PURPOSES. NOTICE
HOW BIG ONE IS.
YOU HAVE TO CHECK
YOUR SPEED &
DISTANCES WHILE
GALLOPING.
WEARS COMPULSORY
MEDICAL INFO ON
ARM. ♥

Karen's scrapbook includes notes about equipment used during the cross-country phase of the World Equestrian Games in Rome, 1998.

69

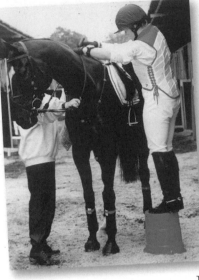

Mounting up at the World Equestrian Games in Rome, 1998

watch them, and top riders such as Mark Todd and Blyth Tait, training.

Merlin continued to improve until, finally, the vet agreed that Karen could also begin to do some schooling work with him. Miraculously, by the first day of competition, Merlin had made a full recovery and was ready to take on the world. Karen, too, was raring to go. Merlin did a decent dressage test, and Karen was reasonably happy with the results as they headed into the cross-country phase.

Despite the heavy going caused by torrential rains, Karen and Merlin had some brilliant moments during their cross-country ride on a course set through the mountains in Italy. Galloping Merlin between fences, Karen thought, *This is what it's all about!*

The exhilaration of her clear ride on the cross-country phase dissipated when Karen realized that Merlin had thrown a

The World Equestrian Games

The FEI World Equestrian Games (WEG) are held every four years. Some equestrians consider these World Championships to be even more significant than the Olympic Games. The equestrian disciplines represented at the WEG are dressage, show jumping, eventing, endurance riding, vaulting, combined driving, and reining. In 2010, the Para-Equestrian World Championships will also be included at the WEG in Lexington, Kentucky. In 2006, the World Equestrian Games were held in Aachen, Germany. More than four dozen countries sent eight hundred riders to compete at the games.

shoe somewhere on the course. The shoe was replaced, but after that Merlin didn't seem himself. He wasn't lame, but Karen sensed there was something wrong.

Before each phase of an eventing competition, horses are jogged in hand. The rider runs alongside the horse while a vet watches to make sure the horse is sound. On the last day of competition, before the stadium jumping phase, Karen and Merlin jogged and the official vet asked for them to be held in the box while Merlin was carefully inspected. Then Karen was asked to jog Merlin out a second time. The crowd began to clap and cheer and Merlin danced and pranced, appearing to float along beside Karen. He passed the vet check in the end, but when Karen mounted she still couldn't shake a feeling of foreboding. She shared her concern with the team groom, Emily Hart, saying, "I don't know what to do — he's not quite right."

Karen was in a difficult situation. Merlin wasn't showing any obvious signs of lameness. If anything, he was only slightly off, and it isn't uncommon for horses competing at this level to be a little footsore after they gallop hard during the endurance phase of an event. Was her horse just feeling the normal effects of the competition? Or was he on the verge of going lame? Merlin was a tough horse with a huge will to compete and do what she asked of him. They had only a handful of jumps left to navigate and

Karen and Merlin during their dressage test at the World Equestrian Games in Rome, 1998.

Karen is all smiles after a clear round on the cross-country course at the World Equestrian Games in Rome, 1998.

then Merlin would have some well-deserved time off. If they withdrew, Karen wouldn't just be disappointed; she would always wonder if she had made the right decision. If she could hang on and finish in the top half, Canada would be allowed to send a rider to the Olympic Games in Sydney in 2000. The fact that Canadian riders were counting on her to have a good round in the stadium jumping just added extra pressure.

"What do you want to do?" Peter Gray asked.

Karen couldn't answer.

"He's your horse," the coach said. "This is your decision. I won't pressure you either way. But if there was ever a moment to push your horse, this is it."

Karen rode Merlin into the warm-up ring. She rode him lightly for less than ten minutes. He popped over four jumps and didn't feel too bad. Karen nodded to Peter Gray. They would go ahead and ride the stadium course.

The jumps in a stadium course aren't nearly as imposing as the obstacles on a cross-country course, but they are still large and much closer together. Horses must constantly change directions, adjust stride length, and make a series of jumping efforts in quick succession. The quick turns and challenging fences are hard on the soft tissues of a horse's legs. The stadium jumping course at the WEG was difficult, and many horses knocked down rails during their rounds.

Entering the ring at a canter, Karen approached the first jump. Merlin caught a rail and knocked it down. Karen's heart sank. When Merlin was in top form, the gutsy horse was a brilliant jumper and rarely knocked anything down.

At the combination of jumps three and four, Karen felt Merlin struggling—he seemed to be having trouble getting off the ground. She hardly had the will to ask Merlin to do anything. Another rail came down and Karen fought to hold back tears. Well into the course, Merlin responded to Karen's requests. With a huge effort, he cleared the final obstacles and left the ring with only two rails down.

Karen's total score placed her fortieth overall, in the top half of the field. Stuart's thirty-second–place finish meant two Canadian riders could travel to Sydney.

Karen's concern, though, had nothing to do with qualifying for Sydney. Outside the ring, she leaped off Merlin's back, distraught. She felt she had ruined her horse, now clearly favouring his left front leg. Though Merlin was examined by the team vet, Dr. Young, in Rome, it was only after she returned to North America and had more complete diagnostic work done that Karen understood the full extent of the damage. Merlin had bowed (pulled) a tendon in his left front leg. The serious injury threatened to end Merlin's jumping career—and Karen's hopes for Olympic glory.

Karen and Merlin clear a vertical in the stadium jumping round at the World Equestrian Games in Rome, 1998.

5

The Fall

Dubbed by Karen the "M+M Event Team," her three horses in 1999 are, left to right, Matzi, Miko, and Merlin. Photo by Fiona Shearer

Merlin's Last Chance

BACK AT THE BARN IN ROME, Karen didn't yet know how bad things were. She hosed down her horse's injured leg with cold water, and Dr. Young gave Merlin his undivided attention. Now that the competition was over, Merlin could be treated with the full range of anti-inflammatory and pain-relief medications. Dr. Young also uses natural remedies, and he pulled out all the stops to make sure that Merlin was soon resting comfortably.

None of this helped Karen, who was in agony. How could she have asked her beloved horse to jump when she had suspected he wasn't quite right? She was afraid of being judged harshly—and didn't she deserve it? What kind of person would sacrifice her horse in order to win? Was winning so important, after all?

Alone in the stall with Merlin, she wrapped her arms around her horse's neck and whispered a promise to him, one she has never broken. "I will never, ever sell you." Her horse had been hurt, but he had come through for her. Despite his illness just before the event and their problems in the show jumping, they had managed to finish in the top half of the field of ninety-two. He deserved all the admiration he was getting; nothing would ever take away his accomplishments. He had taken Karen to the top, and for that Karen was profoundly grateful.

After their return to North America, as Karen grappled with the implications of Merlin's injury, she found herself facing another difficult decision. Should she arrange to have tendon-splitting surgery done on Merlin? It was experimental, but the vet in Virginia who would perform the operation felt there was a chance that, with the surgery, Merlin could make a full recovery. Or should she retire Merlin from competition and keep him comfortable for the rest of his days? After consulting with several vets, Karen decided to go ahead with the surgery.

Several weeks after his operation, Merlin was reassessed. He was much better but still not completely healed. The Virginia vet referred Karen to a colleague in Florida who recommended further treatment, this time a series of injections directly into the tendon. Again, there was a chance the treatment would lead to a full recovery, but there were no guarantees.

Karen consulted again with the Virginia vet who was so familiar with Merlin's case. "What would *you* do?" Karen asked.

The vet felt that Merlin was a rarity, a bona fide four-star-competition horse. "There are maybe two hundred in the world," he said. "If I were you, I'd give him the best possible treatment to try to get that four-star horse back."

Karen nodded. She'd take the risk and hope the end result was positive. By agreeing to the course of injections, she knew she was eliminating herself from competing at the 1999 Pan-Am Games. The series of treatments would first weaken the tendon fibres and then encourage a truer heal. But it would all take time.

For nearly a year, Karen cared for her horse during his long, slow rehabilitation. At the same time, she continued to campaign with Matzi, who was now competing in Advanced horse trials. In 1999 the mare placed in the top twelve at events in Florida, Georgia, North Carolina, and Ontario. In September, Karen and Matzi won at the Glen Oro Horse Trials in the Advanced/Intermediate division. Though Karen had plans to enter Matzi at the Fair Hill cci*** in October, it was not to be. Matzi went lame following an unfortunate shoeing session and was out of commission for three months. When 2000 arrived, Karen took stock: she needed to get out of debt and felt that the time had come to sell the mare, per her original plan. "I was worried I was using her up with each six months I kept her for the next three-day event."

In early 2000, Matzi found a new home in South Carolina and Karen was able to pay back Terri and Rob for their initial investment, some expenses they had covered, plus some interest.

Through the winter of 1999 to 2000 it appeared that Merlin had responded beautifully to treatment, and he started making his comeback. He returned to competition in Thomson, Georgia, in March, finishing fourteenth in the Intermediate division at the Pine Top Horse Trials. After a fourth-place finish in the Advanced Southern Pines Horse Trial in North Carolina, Karen entered Merlin in the North Georgia Beaulieu cic*** event. The pair placed eighteenth. It seemed that Merlin had made a complete recovery so Karen decided to try to qualify for the 2000 Olympic Games and get back on the Canadian team. If she could prove that he could stay sound after competing at another cci*** event in Atlanta, Georgia, in May 2000, Karen and her black horse would qualify for Sydney. Depending on how the other Canadian riders in contention for the two available spots did (and barring any injuries or other unforeseen setbacks), she had a good chance of being notified of her inclusion on the Canadian team shortly before the Olympics.

In May 2000, Merlin seemed fit and strong. He went well in the dressage phase in Atlanta, and Karen and her teammates crossed their fingers as Merlin and Karen headed into the tough endurance day. Toward the end of the steeplechase phase, Karen felt something wasn't quite right. She sensed a slight hesitation as Merlin worked through a figure-eight pattern on hard ground. Three hundred metres before the last jump she hesitated. Two hundred and fifty metres before the jump a thousand thoughts raced through her head. Merlin was moving well, eager and forward. But she had felt something in the figure eight. Was it just the stinging feet so common after this phase? Or was it something more serious?

Karen knew she could ask him for one more jump and he would give it to her. Making that jump would mean they could continue and tackle the cross-country course. If she pulled up, they would be eliminated and she would never know if she had thrown away her chance to compete at the Sydney Olympic Games.

The jump was coming at them. In a moment it would be too late to change her mind. Karen sat back deep in the saddle, pulled up her horse, and walked him past the last jump.

Peter Gray was baffled. "What did you do that for?"

"He's not right," Karen said through tight lips.

An ultrasound done in Atlanta revealed a small tear in the soft tissue of the right front leg and a small lesion in the left. Such tiny aberrations aren't uncommon in horses being worked hard and rarely lead to serious lameness.

Karen found it hard to face the other riders. Had she lost her competitive edge? Top equestrians competing internationally have to struggle with such dilemmas daily. Horses working at this level can't be babied, but how hard should one push them? Like any athlete, the very best riders push hard, striving to attain a slightly better time, a slightly bigger jump. But they owe it to their horses to know when to back off as well.

Six weeks later, Karen asked her friend and vet Dr. Alan Young to do another ultrasound. His careful examination revealed a reinjury of the left tendon as well as a tear in the right front suspensory ligament.

"Tell me if I wasn't justified," she said as they studied the results together.

Dr. Young nodded. "You did the right thing," he said.

His reassurance helped ease Karen's conscience.

During his year off after his injury in Rome, Karen had noticed some subtle changes in Merlin. He wasn't quite as tough and was softer to ride. At fifteen, he wasn't a young horse anymore. When Karen rode past the final jump in Atlanta, she knew that Merlin could no longer be a top-level eventer. They would never go to the Olympics together.

Miko: Agent of Fate

Without Merlin, Karen was once again without a top-notch horse capable of carrying her in international competition. She was now based near London in southern Ontario and was having some success with a friend's horse, Ruba Z. Karen rode the striking dapple grey to several top-four finishes at lower level competitions including a first at the Glen Oro CCI* in Ontario in 2000.

The year before, Karen had bought a young horse called Miko in Florida. She had hoped she could train and develop him as she had Merlin, Matzi, and Alpo. Despite the fact she hadn't initially liked Miko and had not felt an immediate strong emotional connection with him, she had talked herself into the purchase. Her ambivalence about her decision to buy Miko is reflected in the show name she chose for him: Second Thought.

She had been working with Miko for over a year when Merlin went lame, but he was still feisty and argumentative and hadn't made much progress. Hypersensitive, he behaved at times like an unbroken horse. He was also intermittently lame (Miko had much preferred the sandy footing of Florida to the harder ground surface in Ontario), which made his training even more difficult.

By the fall of 2001, these ongoing soundness problems and his lack of progress under saddle persuaded Karen to prepare the horse for sale. She would then be back in the hunt for another horse with international potential.

During the afternoon of September 18, 2001, Karen was well into a particularly frustrating ride on Miko when she heard someone behind her say, "Karen, you are going to fall off today."

She turned around to see who had spoken, but the riding ring was empty.

Karen decided to try to end the lesson on a good note by taking the horse out into the field for a relaxed trot. Once outside the confines of the riding ring, Miko seemed to settle down. Karen rode along a path in the woods where she knew there was a little jump across the trail. If she could get Miko to hop over the jump, they would have accomplished something positive and she could call it a day.

Miko, though, had other ideas. When he felt Karen's legs on his sides he ran sideways through the trees, oblivious to the fact he could easily have knocked his rider out of the saddle. Karen pulled him up and decided that a nice, well-behaved walk back to the barn would suffice. She wasn't going to get into a big fight with Miko just to make him go over the jump.

Miko didn't want anything to do with a well-behaved walk, even if it was back toward the barn. He ignored Karen's leg aids to move forward, planted his feet, and balked. Karen gave him a kick and he pinned his ears and swished his tail.

Now both horse and rider were irritated. Karen swatted the end of the reins across the recalcitrant horse's neck, trying to get him to go forward. He leaped straight up and landed stiff-legged. Karen sat tight and said, "That didn't get you far, did it?"

Karen and her boyfriend, Rob Close, at a wedding in August 2001.

She asked him to move forward again and this time he jumped sideways. Instinctively, Karen held on to the reins in an effort to stay on, but by pulling his head and neck to one side as he leaped into the air, she threw Miko off balance. Miko crashed over sideways as he landed, and Karen felt the great mass of horse crumple and fall. There was nothing Karen could do to get out of the way, no time to jump clear or protect herself. Miko landed almost upside down, rolling sideways. His momentum carried him onto his back and he pinned Karen underneath him, driving her knees into her chest.

Miko scrambled to his feet and headed back to the barn. Lying in the dirt on her back, Karen pushed up until she was supporting her upper body on her elbows. She could not move her legs and had no feeling below her waist. She knew immediately that she had broken her back, and all the implications of such an injury hit her. Instead of panicking, Karen found herself completely calm. In the few minutes it took for the first people to come to her aid, she scolded herself.

"Way to go, Karen. Now look what you've done. You're never going to be able to walk again. You'll never run, dance, drive—or ride—again. What are you going to do with the rest of your life?" When the first people from the barn reached her side she said, "Call 911. I've broken my back."

The uninjured muscles in Karen's body constricted in powerful, painful spasms. A natural defence mechanism, the locked muscles helped keep Karen's body still and limit further injury. Karen knew she shouldn't move, so with the support of two young women from the barn, she endured the agonizing spasms and waited for the ambulance.

Once she was in the hospital emergency room, the excruciating pain intensified with every minute she waited for medical attention. She moaned aloud, "Why won't anybody help me? I've broken my back. Please, somebody help me."

It wasn't until her boyfriend, Rob Close, arrived more than thirty minutes later that things began to happen. When he realized she still hadn't been X-rayed, he stormed to the admitting desk and demanded to know when Karen would receive treatment. His fury and Karen's increasingly loud groans of agony did the trick. Karen was immediately X-rayed and they realized that she had indeed broken her back. Things moved quickly after that. Karen was rushed off to a second hospital where more X-rays were taken. It was only then that doctors understood the extent of the damage.

Surgery and Reconstruction

Karen was finally given powerful painkillers and she gratefully sank into a groggy haze, relieved to be free of the intense pain for the first time since the accident. Her T12 vertebra, which is approximately at the level of the base of the rib cage, was completely destroyed—the impact had shattered it and sent tiny splinters everywhere. Surgery was needed to remove these shards, and a special titanium bone cage had to be built around the T11 and L1 vertebrae (located on either side of the destroyed area). Doctors would have to construct a new T12 inside the cage, using bone from one of Karen's ribs.

Before Karen underwent the surgery, she received a relatively new treatment. With spinal cord injuries, it's essential to begin treatment quickly. The body's natural response to injury is to send fluid to the damaged area. Inside the tight, enclosed space of the spinal column, though, there is no room for swelling. Pressure on healthy tissue can severely damage it, and it may never recover. Down the road, this can mean additional loss of function. Some researchers and doctors believe that administering large doses of the powerful steroid methylprednisolene can reduce the swelling and minimize this collateral damage. Despite the shock of the accident, her pain, and the importance of the decision, Karen felt the potential benefits were worth the risks and agreed to the treatment.

Karen received the medication for thirty-six hours. Then it was stopped and she had to wait another thirty-six hours before it was safe to proceed with her surgery. Karen's parents scrambled to find plane tickets to get them to Ontario—not an easy feat just a week after the September 11 attacks in New York.

The hours passed slowly as Karen waited for surgery. Despite medications, the pain was relentless. To prevent bedsores, every so often nurses turned Karen from one side to the other, a process Karen dreaded. Even the lightest touch on her skin, at least in areas where she had any sensation, seemed like a million needles stabbing her flesh.

To help prevent her lower legs from swelling and developing blood clots, Karen wore tight, elastic, tension stockings. She couldn't use a bedpan, so she was catheterized, a procedure where a small tube is inserted to drain the bladder. When Karen realized a catheter meant that nobody would try to

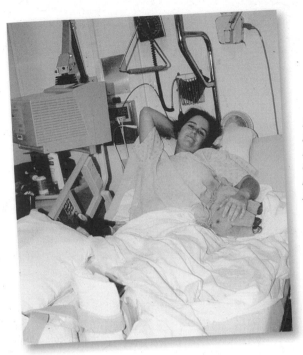

Karen in her hospital bed in London, Ontario, a few days after her surgery in 2001.

move her when she needed to relieve herself, she didn't care about the indignity.

Word of Karen's injury spread fast and the day after her accident, while she waited for surgery, visitors crowded into her hospital room. When Karen's parents arrived after their long flight from British Columbia, they walked into a completely unexpected scene. They had steeled themselves for the worst, fully expecting Karen to be devastated and depressed. Instead, a dozen riding friends surrounded Karen's bed, and laughter and chatter filled the room. Flowers and cards covered every surface, and Karen greeted her mom and dad with a huge grin.

"What great timing!" she said. "Now you can meet all my friends from London!"

Darlene tried to smile, though, in truth, meeting Karen's friends was about the last thing in the world that she felt like doing. Darlene was shocked at how happy Karen seemed as she laughed with her friends and introduced everyone.

The cheery break with friends was a wonderful tonic for Karen. Soon enough, she and her family would experience the kinds of extreme challenges families hope they will never face.

As Karen and her family waited out the thirty-six hours needed for the steroids to clear from her system, the reality of what the surgeons were about to do sank in. Karen began to feel nervous. Alone with her parents at her side the night before the operation, she broke down and wept. She apologized for causing everyone so much trouble and making them worry.

"Mom?" she asked, crying. "What if something happens during the operation? What if I don't survive?"

Darlene answered with a confidence she didn't feel. "You'll come out of this just fine. You are strong and determined. Everything will be okay."

Through her tears Karen said, "You've got to promise me that if anything happens to me you'll find a good home for my horses—Miko, too."

Squeezing her daughter's hand, Darlene said, "Karen, you know we love you so much. You're going to come through with flying colours." Darlene could hardly speak when she added, "But we promise to look after Merlin and Miko."

Seeing the stricken look on his daughter's face, Bill also tried to reassure her. "Don't worry. We'll take care of them. We love you."

It was late and all three of them were exhausted. Karen needed to try to rest before the ordeal that lay ahead. "We'll see you in the morning," Bill said. Despite their best efforts to remain upbeat and optimistic, nobody slept well that night as visions of all the things that could go wrong tormented each of them.

The next day dragged by for Karen's parents in the hospital waiting room. Karen's team of surgeons carefully

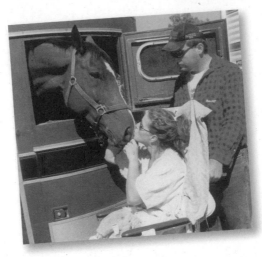

In the immediate aftermath of the accident, Karen was furious with Miko (pictured with Karen in late September 2001). "If I had been coherent and had a phone handy, I would have arranged for the meat van to come and take him away," she confesses. But very quickly she forgave the horse, accepting that she ultimately had to take responsibility for what had happened. "I had to get over my anger, let go of it. He just reacted the way horses sometimes react and, just like a mother whose child has done something bad, I had to forgive him and love him anyway."

reconstructed her shattered spine. They also discovered that one of Karen's lungs had been collapsed by the force of Karen's knees driving into her chest when Miko had fallen on her. Karen's superb fitness and positive attitude had completely masked the fact that she was breathing with only one lung!

Finally, seven and a half hours after doctors made the first incision, Bill and Darlene were paged and taken into another room to speak with several of Karen's doctors.

"Except for the lung, everything went exactly as planned!" they were told. Inserting a tube to drain fluid from the collapsed lung had been an unexpected, but successful, extra procedure.

That the surgery had gone well was good news, but nobody could tell Bill and Darlene exactly what the outcome of the "successful" operation would be. At thirty-one, Karen was a paraplegic; only time would tell how much function she would eventually regain below the level of her injury. And nobody could have prepared Bill and Darlene for what they saw when they stepped into the intensive care ward to see their daughter for the first time after the operation.

Still unconscious, Karen was pale and silent. Tubes stuck out everywhere. An intravenous needle disappeared into her jugular vein. Monitors beeped and blipped. Fluids and medications dripped through an IV needle into her arm. A horrible greenish yellow substance was being suctioned out of her lung through another tube. Darlene could not look at her husband or at Karen's friend Fiona Shearer, afraid that meeting their eyes would release a flood of tears. Instead, she looked at her broken daughter and hoped that somehow they would all find the strength to face whatever lay ahead. Later, Fiona told Darlene that after seeing Karen lying motionless and unconscious, she had sat in her car in the parking lot and wept, horrified.

Rob, too, spent many hours at Karen's side, offering whatever support he could.

What Happens After a Spinal Cord Injury?

In a spinal cord injury, the nerves sending messages to the muscles below the level of the injury are permanently damaged. Generally, the higher up the spinal column the injury occurs, the more muscle groups are affected. If the cord is completely destroyed, the result is complete paralysis below the injury. If the message sent from the brain that tells a particular muscle to contract cannot get past the damaged area, the muscle cannot contract, can't be used, and can't be strengthened. In cases like Karen's (considered incomplete paraplegia), some nerve fibres survive the initial break and some function below the damage is eventually recovered. Each of the muscle groups in Karen's legs was affected a little differently, with damage being much worse in some areas than others and different on each side of the body.

Karen drifted in and out of consciousness, aware of a distant pain in her side, the result of the long incision made to remove the rib used to rebuild her vertebra. The heavy sedation and pain medications caused strange hallucinations. Once, Karen watched in horror as a black bug crawled out of her mother's tear duct and scuttled over her face. *I can't believe that's not bothering her,* Karen thought. She watched the beetle, fascinated. *Maybe it's not there and I'm hallucinating,* she mused.

Then she slipped back into a deep sleep.

Cards and flowers fill Karen's hospital room in September 2001.

6

The Slow Road to Recovery

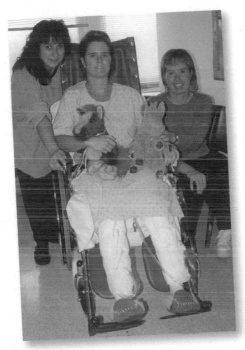

Karen had no shortage of visitors while she was in the hospital. From left to right, Terri (Karen's sister), Karen, and Elizabeth Safranyik (Karen's friend).

BIT BY BIT OVER THE NEXT TWO DAYS the nurses removed equipment that Karen no longer needed. With throat and nose tubes gone and the IV taken out of her neck, all Karen had left was the chest tube and an IV drip into one hand. What a huge relief it was to be able to talk normally!

Breathing was another question. Daily therapy helped improve her lung capacity, though Karen found the relentless rounds of physiotherapy painful and annoying. Exhausted and aching, all she wanted to do was sleep. But post-surgical recovery is forced along at lightning speed. The current philosophy is to get patients up and moving as quickly as possible to stimulate circulation, promote healing, prevent post-operative complications such as blood clots, and allow for a quick start on physiotherapy. Implementing a physiotherapy program helps ward off problems such as shrinking muscles and tendons and, ultimately, maximizes the eventual amount of function regained following a spinal cord injury. The fact it was good for Karen did little to make the process easier.

Karen's sister, Terri, and her childhood friend Elizabeth Safranyik flew to Ontario to be with Karen for a few days, and seeing them meant a great deal to her.

Each day the nurses and rehabilitation staff asked Karen to do more and more. By the end of the third day, with an assistant on each side, Karen was propped up in bed. It was torture to try to balance upright. Waves of nausea threatened to overwhelm her and she found that she had no balance at all. She couldn't hold herself in a sitting position, and after only a few minutes she dripped with sweat and her heart pounded—and all she had done was sit still!

The therapists were relentless, and with each visit Karen was able to sit up for just a little longer. After another day or two the nurses transferred Karen to a wheelchair, though her wooziness prevented her from staying there for long.

Terri, Elizabeth, and Karen's parents watched that first time as Karen was lifted into a wheelchair. Then the girls took charge and pushed Karen over to the window in a nearby waiting room.

Karen's mother vividly recalls the scene. "The tears were just pouring down my face with the reality and sadness of it all. I tried not to let Karen see me cry, and I don't think she did." It was one of the few times Darlene cried at the hospital.

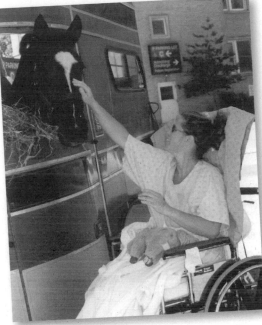

Karen visits with Merlin in the parking lot of the hospital eleven days after her accident.

As Karen began to feel better, she threw herself into her physiotherapy with characteristic determination. Like that of most riders, Karen's upper body was strong from years of tossing hay bales, shovelling manure, and endlessly repeating the give and take adjustments made by the shoulders, arms, and hands when riding a horse. Though finesse is the name of the game during a dressage test, controlling a five-hundred-kilogram horse's stride during a cross-country gallop requires tremendous strength and coordination. An excited horse in top condition can pull hard, and an effective rider has considerable core and upper body strength. Though she had no feeling and could not control any muscles below her waist, Karen supported her weight with her arms when she first "stood" between a set of parallel bars within a week of her surgery.

The external symptoms of a spinal cord injury are apparent to onlookers, but just as serious are problems with paralysis of the internal muscles that control bladder and bowel function. Before Karen was allowed to leave the hospital where she'd had her surgery and move to Parkwood Rehabilitation Hospital in London, Ontario, all her internal systems needed to be working smoothly. Medication started things moving, but bowel troubles were an ongoing aggravation.

As the days passed, Karen grew antsy. She couldn't wait to get started on her specialized therapy. She assumed she would be in the rehabilitation hospital for a few weeks at most. When she learned that she would be a resident at Parkwood at least until Christmas, she was floored. When she was told that outpatient rehabilitation could go on for several years, she was shocked. Her idea of recovery did not include years of hospital visits.

During the first weeks after surgery, doctors steadfastly refused to speculate on the level of function Karen might eventually regain. "I'm glad I didn't really know the full extent of the damage," she says about the lack of information early on. "Initially, I just assumed I would walk again." Had she known that some people who have had the same injury and the identical surgery never leave their wheelchairs, she might have found it more difficult to throw herself into physiotherapy with such determination and enthusiasm.

As it was, on October 1, 2001, Karen left the primary care hospital and moved into Parkwood Rehabilitation Hospital, determined to be the best patient they'd ever seen!

Therapy started immediately, and it was hard work, though not nearly as bad as Karen had feared. Before her accident, Karen had regularly put in sixteen-hour days of hard physical labour. She was more than able to do whatever her new therapists asked of her. The rewards, though hard won and not dramatic, began soon after her arrival.

One day as she was lying in her hospital bed late in October, Karen had the distinct feeling that one of her toes had moved. She mentioned this to Rob, who leaped out of his chair, whipped the sheet off Karen's legs, and demanded, "Do it again! Make them move!"

Karen concentrated hard and tried again and, sure enough, they both saw the slightest movement of one toe. Both Karen and Rob burst into tears and couldn't stop smiling. Karen sent Rob off to find one of the nurses. "I was so excited!"

Karen remembers. "I couldn't wait to show someone from the medical profession, to get their take on what it meant."

When Darlene and Bill came back to the room a few minutes later, they knew right away something significant had happened. "Come and see this!" Karen said, her eyes still brimming with tears.

Cheers and more tears followed, and the nurses roundly congratulated Karen for achieving a milestone. But the best news came from her surgeon, who saw her about two weeks later. When Karen pointed to her foot and demonstrated her toe twitch, a big smile warmed his face and he said, "Karen— do you know what this means?"

Karen shook her head. "What?"

"This means you will walk again."

Karen was overjoyed. It hardly seemed possible that such an amazing recovery could be predicted by the tiny movement of one toe, but Karen took the doctor's words to heart and doubled her efforts in her physiotherapy sessions. If she could walk again, then surely she'd also ride again. Though filled with renewed hope and optimism, Karen was still blissfully ignorant about just how hard it would be to get from the small movement of a toe to being able to walk on her own again.

While Karen settled into her new life at Parkwood, she still needed to work at getting her sluggish plumbing to

Karen visits the barn not long after her surgery, 2001.

come back to life. During the first two weeks, Karen spent many long hours sitting on the toilet, waiting for something to happen. To keep her company, Darlene pulled up a chair and sat beside her. It was in this odd location that mother and daughter shared some long and profound conversations.

It is not uncommon for people who have suffered a spinal cord injury to experience some depression as they come to accept their new status, physical limitations, and increased dependency on others. But Karen's experience was quite different. Part of the reason was that Karen couldn't shake the idea that she had been gearing up for a change. Even though she was upset and exhausted and found it a struggle to do the simplest things, like sit up or take a deep breath, her dominant emotional state was relief. "A big part of me was happy to be in the hospital," Karen confesses.

There were three reasons for this unlikely attitude. First, she was just plain tired: tired of struggling to make ends meet, tired of being stressed out about not knowing where her next good horse would come from, and tired of worrying about keeping her horses fit and sound under the strain of hard competition. She loved the break from her usual onerous routine of horse care and training from sunrise to sunset. Karen had been ready to make a shift for some time and had been considering going back to school, so to be in a hospital was at least a change, albeit not exactly the one she had been contemplating.

Second, all previous expectations that others had for her— and that she had for herself—suddenly disappeared. Other people were in charge of making the decisions regarding her health and recovery. Karen, and not her horses, was the subject of a carefully planned program, and she loved the luxury of not being the one doing all the thinking all the time. The only thing Karen had to do was get better.

The third reason she wasn't more traumatized about the accident became clearer over time. "Looking back on it now, it was almost as if at the moment of the accident I was put onto my true life's path," Karen explains. "I always had a sense that one day I would have to face something that would test me, that I would have to survive a great hardship. I put myself on that horse and took full responsibility for what happened, and I never fought that. It was like I had seen the accident coming, and when it actually happened, I recognized it."

With her parents close by, Karen also reflected on just how critical it was to have family and friends in her life. Without people she loved, she realized, she had nothing. Karen had always appreciated the support and encouragement she had received from her family, but until her body was damaged she didn't realize just how profoundly important her loved ones were.

"I had always been a very independent person—I drove my truck and trailer to events, I groomed my own horses, I made plans and decisions, found jobs—and I loved my friends and my family. But I didn't fully appreciate how they enhanced my life. You can win gold—but without those people to share it with, the triumph isn't as meaningful."

Karen never fought against the idea that others had to help her with her recovery. "I knew the seriousness of my injury." She certainly didn't want to injure herself again by trying to do too much too soon, or by being proud and not accepting help. "I had to let others take care of me." She was deeply grateful that there were people around her who were willing to put their lives on hold to help her heal.

Karen sometimes had physiotherapy sessions in the therapy pool at the hospital. Because she couldn't control her legs, they would occasionally do strange things in the water. In one exercise, Karen had to stand in the pool, using the water and her natural buoyancy to help her stay upright. Karen couldn't feel what her legs were doing, and it was hard to see her feet at the bottom of the pool, so she had her toenails painted fluorescent pink. If she lost her balance at all, her feet, led by those bright pink toenails, slowly rose to the surface in front of Karen. "Watch out! Here they come!" she would shout as she started to tip over.

Exercises outside the pool focused first on standing and eventually on retraining Karen's muscles in the complicated sequence of movements required for walking. With therapists supporting her, Karen laboured each day to learn to stand by herself. After weeks of effort, she was able to stand without human assistance, using canes with curved handles for balance.

It took much longer to coax her legs to move on their own. Two helpers stood, one on either side of her, to hold her up, and another crouched on the floor, moving each of Karen's feet in turn. Karen couldn't tell her muscles to contract, so a fourth person behind her goosed her backside to force the muscles to respond. A fifth helper followed close behind with a wheelchair in case Karen collapsed. Hundreds and hundreds of times, helpers guided her feet, knees, and thighs to move each leg through each step.

It wasn't at all strange for Karen to be at the centre of a circle of people who were helping her get where she was going, and she saw this new team of professionals as her allies. She enjoyed the good humour, hard work, and knowledge of the physiotherapy team and understood it was by forming a strong alliance with these professionals that she could get the most from her therapy sessions.

In some areas below her injury, Karen had no sensation or movement at all. In other areas, she experienced strange sensations and hypersensitivity depending on the degree of damage to the nerves at the level of her break. The damage was uneven, so her left side was much more sensitive than her right.

Medication helped keep the pain at bay as she healed, allowing Karen to do the various types of therapy. A patient can't function well unless the pain is controlled. The effect of pain is as much psychological as physical. When Karen was feeling comfortable, she wasn't afraid to try to do whatever was asked of her. But when the medication wore off and the pain returned, Karen became anxious, fearful that she had done too much or moved in the wrong way and reinjured herself.

Frequent rest periods and carefully planned sequences of increasingly difficult exercises were built into her routine and, bit by bit, she was rewarded with small signs of improvement.

During the first weeks after her arrival at Parkwood, Karen met with all the members of her medical team to discuss her progress and fine-tune her rehabilitation program. At the first meeting, she was shocked at how many people sat around the conference room table. Nearly two dozen health care professionals discussed every aspect of Karen's care and recovery.

When it was her turn to ask questions, Karen wanted to know one thing more than any other. "When can I ride again?" she asked, confident that her excellent progress would mean a quick return to the saddle. She knew there was some sort of team for disabled riders that competed internationally, including at the Paralympic Games, and she was eager to begin participating.

A physician who was a specialist in spinal cord injuries answered the question. "About a year."

"What?! No, really—how long will it be?"

Karen takes a day trip to Rob's farm within a few weeks of her surgery in 2001.

"About a year," he repeated. "You must appreciate the severity of your injury..." He continued to speak, as did others around the table, but Karen heard none of them.

All she could hear was the voice in her head saying, "Don't cry. Don't cry. Don't cry. At least wait until you're out of the room."

At last the meeting ended and Karen fled, a nurse pushing her chair down the hall and back to her room. Karen could hardly breathe, she was crying so hard. Sobbing and hyperventilating, she managed to gasp out what the doctor had said. Her parents and the nurse tried to soothe her. They told her that waiting a year was just a sensible preventive measure.

Gradually, Karen collected herself and began to think more clearly. She could barely hold herself upright and was constantly terrified of toppling over sideways. Riding in a car, she couldn't handle going around corners. Sitting on a moving horse really was out of the question. Her lung still wasn't healed—she couldn't fully expand her chest to draw a proper breath. The pain she felt everywhere wasn't going to go away just because she was on top of a horse. If anything, it would be much worse.

It wasn't easy, but Karen had to accept the fact she was not going to get on a horse for a very long time. And if she were completely honest, she would admit she might *never* regain enough mobility, strength, and balance to ride again. As for competition, well, that was beginning to seem like a most unlikely dream.

For the first time in her life, Karen pushed aside all thoughts of horses and riding and put together a different set of goals. She was going to stand by herself without canes. She was going to walk. She was going to dance. That would be enough.

7

Double Take

Having friends and family close by means a lot to Karen during her recovery.
Photo by Bill Brain

Back in the Saddle

TINY IMPROVEMENTS FROM WEEK to week kept Karen working hard in her physiotherapy sessions. One week she might struggle and struggle to tell her leg to move to the side, with no visible result except her panting and sweating. A therapist would move the leg for her, repeating the motion many times, day after day. The following week the leg shifted a centimetre to the side, though Karen had no sensation

Karen during her visit to B.C. at Christmas 2001.

of that movement. Therapists repeated the motion many, many more times. The following week the motion was two centimetres and Karen experienced some sensation along with the action. And so it went, week after week, with all the muscle groups in her hips, lower back, and legs being prodded, squeezed, poked, moved, and manipulated as she struggled to make her muscles do what they were supposed to do.

After two and a half months of intensive daily therapy at Parkwood, Karen was making excellent progress. With the help of leg braces and two canes she was able to shuffle around for short distances under her own steam. But generally she used her wheelchair and a walker in the hospital, unable to last long on her feet.

Her parents had returned home in November and Karen couldn't wait to see them again. She was discharged from Parkwood on December 13, 2001, and flew home for a month-long visit over Christmas. She arrived with her wheelchair, a walker, two canes, cumbersome leg braces, and a list of instructions for looking after herself without the daily support of hospital staff.

Of course, many of Karen's friends rode and she couldn't resist making expeditions to local barns. Watching her friend Glynis Schultz jumping her horse, Ngapuhi, Karen felt a familiar desire stirring. Glynis guided Ngapuhi over several jumps during a training session, and a voice that Karen had been repressing made itself heard again. She really did want to ride again, just to prove to herself that she could do it.

Karen and her family discussed the possibility of a move back to British Columbia, but there was no rehabilitation centre equivalent to Parkwood on Vancouver Island, and Karen wasn't interested in moving to Vancouver. She wasn't even keen on extending her Christmas holiday. She knew that there is a window of opportunity that lasts about two years after a spinal cord injury. It is during this time that the average patient regains whatever function they are likely to regain. She couldn't see much point in lying around on the couch watching TV when she could be back in her rehabilitation program making the most of every day available to her.

After her month in British Columbia, Karen returned to Ontario where she resumed her physiotherapy program as an outpatient. Karen moved back into the rented room where she had been living prior to the accident. Two students leased Merlin, helping cover his costs, and Miko had been sold. Karen was able to earn a little money by teaching riding lessons, sitting at the side of the ring in her wheelchair to instruct her students.

Karen, her friend Fiona, and a curious cat in the fall of 2001.

But she certainly couldn't return to the kind of work schedule she had always kept in the past.

In March 2002, at her six-month checkup, Karen sat opposite her surgeon as he examined her X-rays and read over reports from Parkwood. Vowing to do exactly what she was told, Karen couldn't resist asking, "So, when do you think I might be able to start riding again?"

To her surprise, her doctor met her gaze and said, "I suppose some slow flatwork might be possible."

"When?"

"Now."

Karen nearly fell off her chair with surprise. "Now?"

"No jumping."

Karen didn't argue. She hadn't expected to be in a saddle again for another six months. Slow flatwork sounded wonderful.

The night before she was to go to the barn, Karen could hardly sleep. She imagined that she would feel a sense of euphoria and a grand feeling of recovery. She expected that a rush of emotions would overwhelm her when she sat astride Merlin for the first time in so long. She pictured herself with her arms slung in blissful gratitude around her horse's neck.

The reality of the following day was quite different. Mounting, at least, wasn't too bad; she had always trained her horses to move close to, and stand quietly beside, the mounting block. She hung on to the stirrup leather for balance, carefully climbed the three steps of the mounting block, and pulled herself up into the saddle. (Later, Karen also taught her horses to help her after she dismounted. They learned to back alongside the mounting block while she held the stirrup leather and climbed down the steps, and they stayed beside her until she was safely on the ground again.)

But once on Merlin's back, Karen was shocked at how hard it was just to sit in the saddle. It was beyond uncomfortable— it was excruciatingly painful. Even at a walk, with Rob leading Merlin, Karen felt wobbly and awkward. Her balance was completely off, and pain shot through her ankles when she put her feet in the stirrups.

"Let's try on the lunge line," Karen suggested. Maybe it would be easier at the trot. This hopeful thought disappeared with Merlin's first strides. Posting was impossible and sitting the trot agonizing. *This really sucks*, Karen thought. So much for euphoria.

Completely frustrated, Karen asked for a canter. It was a little easier to deal with than the bouncy trot, but she could still manage only half a circle before she pulled Merlin to a stop. Her ankles hurt, so she dropped her feet out of her stirrups and rode for a few minutes more at the walk. But even going slowly, with her legs hanging loosely at Merlin's sides, the effort to stay aboard was huge and exhausting.

"That was pathetic," she said after her awkward dismount. She gave Merlin a pat and an apple and told him, "We have a lot of work to do."

Riding again, no matter how badly, told Karen several things. First, she knew she would not be happy riding just for fun. She was too competitive for that. But, to be competitive again, she needed to be strong enough to stay aboard for more than five minutes. She needed to be able to put her feet in the stirrups. If she couldn't post, she had to be able to sit. If she was going to sit to her horse's movement properly, she needed to find a new way to balance with her altered body. Many of the muscle groups in her lower back, buttocks, and legs had wasted away and no longer worked the way they once did. No matter how much therapy she did each day, they would never be as strong as they had been.

With some feeling and movement gradually returning to her legs, Karen was now considered to be an "incomplete paraplegic." Doctors still refused to indicate how much function she might eventually recover. The official medical line was that her ultimate degree of recovery depended a lot on how much effort she put into her physiotherapy and that most patients reach a plateau after two years of treatment.

At about this time, Karen decided to pursue her interest in Para-Equestrian dressage competition. She wondered how on earth competitions for disabled riders were kept fair. Some riders, she knew, were blind; others were missing limbs. Yet others were complete paraplegics with more severe damage to the spinal cord than she had experienced. Though Karen had

learned that riders with her level of disability and those facing even more difficult challenges competed at dressage competitions around the world, she wasn't sure how they managed

Karen gallops on Wink in 2002, less than a year after her accident.
Photo by Rob Close

to convey the subtle signals to their horses to execute the complex patterns of dressage tests. She also had no idea how one qualified for the Para-Equestrian team.

Just as she had done when she wanted to find out about the national eventing team, Karen got on the phone. She asked what she had to do to compete on the Para-Equestrian team and was told that, first, she needed to get classified by a physiotherapist accredited to evaluate Para-Equestrian athletes. Karen soon understood how competition between riders with different disabilities is kept fair: riders with similar levels of disability compete in classes against each other. Within each class or grade, scores are calculated purely on how well the horse and rider execute the dressage test, exactly in the same way scores are calculated and competitions are judged for able-bodied riders.

Receiving a Grade I, II, III, or IV designation would be one aspect of Karen's new life as a disabled athlete. The second dimension of team competition was determining the athlete's riding ability. To ride on the Canadian team, Karen had to achieve scores in dressage high enough to qualify her for competition at the international level.

"If I can get classified and all that," Karen said during her phone conversation with a Para-Equestrian team administrator, "how quickly could I be on the team? Where will they be competing next?"

The Para-Equestrian team was planning to travel to Portugal in September 2002 to compete at the European Championships for Disabled Riders. The event was a few short months away. Karen couldn't post and couldn't ride at the trot for more than two or three minutes. The pain in her left ankle was so bad she couldn't use a stirrup at all. But to Karen, the European Championships in September seemed like an entirely reasonable goal. If she did well there, she'd go on to the World Championships the following year, and

Disabled Athletes in Competition

Disabled athletes compete in as many as six disability categories: amputee, cerebral palsy, intellectual disability, Les Autres (various locomotor conditions such as multiple sclerosis), vision impairment, and wheelchair. Not all disability categories are allowed in each sport. Within each category, athletes are assigned a grade corresponding to the individual's level of impairment. Each sport divides disabled athletes into groups with similar levels of impairment. In the case of team competitions, like basketball, rules ensure that each team has a balance of more and less severely disabled participants.

In equestrian competition, riders are grouped in four grades, as follows:

- **Grade I.** Severely disabled riders with cerebral palsy, Les Autres, and spinal cord injury.
- **Grade II.** Amputees and athletes with cerebral palsy, Les Autres, and spinal cord injury involving less severe impairment than Grade I.
- **Grade III.** Totally blind riders and those from the cerebral palsy, amputee, and spinal cord injury groups who have good balance, leg movement, and coordination. This is the grade assigned to Karen when she was first classified.
- **Grade IV.** Athletes with this designation are ambulant (able to walk) and may belong to any of the categories. Visually impaired riders with some impaired arm or leg function are considered to be Grade IV athletes. When Karen was reclassified in 2004, she was given a Grade IV designation.

Riders with improving or deteriorating conditions must be re-evaluated within six months of the WEG or the Paralympic Games.

Dressage competitions for disabled riders started in Scandinavia and Great Britain in the 1970s, but it wasn't until Atlanta in 1996 that equestrian sport was included in the Paralympic Games. Riders now compete under rules set by the international governing body for equestrian sport, the FEI.

---

the year after that the 2004 Paralympic Games in Athens beckoned. There was no time to lose. Karen had to get to work. "I can do that," she said. "I can be ready."

After hanging up the phone, Karen wondered what she had just done. Setting herself such a difficult goal would do one of two things: either push her along and help her recovery, or drive her to an early grave.

Karen threw herself at her new project with her usual optimism and pigheaded determination. She learned to sit deeper in the saddle and rely on balance more than she ever had before. Classified as a Grade III rider, Karen was allowed to ride with certain assistive devices—two dressage whips, one in each hand, and special elastics to help keep her feet in the stirrups—if she decided to use them. The light tap of a whip helped replace the aid she would normally have given with her leg, and special wedge-shaped stirrup treads helped ease the agonizing pain in her ankles by keeping them from flexing.

Karen struggled to do two-point cantering to improve her own fitness and to help her get her heels down into a better position. The two-point work also helped strengthen her ankles. Though Karen had some use of muscles in her thighs and buttocks (used for maintaining position in the saddle), they were much weaker and, in certain cases, non-functional. They were also unreliable, not responding in quite the same way they had prior to her injury. Her horses had to learn how to respond quickly to much lighter aids than they had in the past. While Karen was working hard to retrain herself to ride in a new way, she was also working hard to retrain her mounts.

And Karen rode a lot, pushing herself to the point of pain and exhaustion and then just a little beyond. She started riding two horses a day, riding one horse without stirrups for dressage work and the second horse with shorter stirrups for fitness and Achilles tendon stretching. When she could no longer hold herself in the saddle, she walked her horse in hand, leading Merlin. When she tumbled over in the uneven footing of the riding ring, she consoled herself that at least the landing was soft.

Karen's progress in the riding ring was matched by her ongoing outpatient sessions at Parkwood. Day by day she grew stronger and her stamina increased.

Though her physiotherapy was going well, getting on the national Para-Equestrian team proved to be difficult. The number of spots available on the team was limited. Canada wanted to send the best team possible to Europe, and every effort had to be made to ensure the selection process was fair. There was no way to base Karen's current abilities on what she had accomplished before her injury. She needed to be judged and scored in appropriate shows.

Entries for larger shows often close well in advance of the show date and one Ontario show Karen tried to enter simply refused to let her compete. She had managed to get the necessary health approvals for her horse, obtain the appropriate club membership, and dig out her horse's passport, the identification document that lists show results and vaccination and health records. But the show entry date had passed and no amount of pleading and explaining would change the organizers' minds.

After she explained her dilemma to the Canadian team officials, arrangements were made to have Karen ride in a show in front of two qualified judges. If Karen's scores for the championship test and Kur (a freestyle dressage test ridden to music) were high enough to qualify for the international competition in Portugal, she then had to arrange to ride in front of a second set of judges. This second set of scores would also have to meet the standards. After all these criteria were met, team officials would still have to decide if Karen was going to be an asset to the Canadian team.

While she prepared for her dressage tests, Karen increased the amount of time she spent at the barn. She rode at least twice a day, both Merlin and a student's horse, Wink, with whom she'd begun competing shortly before her accident. Several times a week she worked out at the gym and went to physiotherapy. Karen continued to teach her students and picked up a bit of part-time office work at the hospital.

One day she was holding Merlin while the farrier trimmed the horse's feet and put on new shoes. Noting that Karen looked white as a ghost, the farrier asked her if she needed to sit down.

"I'm just really, really tired," she said.

There were plenty of days like that, when the last thing she felt like doing was climbing on a horse, but she did it anyway. On the weekends when there was no physiotherapy, Karen slept and slept and slept, her aching muscles recovering from the brutal regime she had established. At night, painful muscle cramps sometimes made her feet go rigid. As an athlete preparing for international competition, Karen had to get special permission to take a muscle relaxant each night to help with this problem.

Difficult though the long days were, Karen was happy to have a goal and delighted to see that she was accomplishing something with all her hours of physiotherapy and training. After each weekend of sleeping and resting she found that she was stronger on Monday and able to do a bit more than she had the week before.

Soon she was able to stay in the saddle longer and ask more and more of her horse. Her endurance and strength improved steadily and, correspondingly, her confidence grew. Karen pushed herself even harder.

Merlin seemed to sense that something was up with his rider. He was easier to handle and more relaxed. When Karen slumped in the saddle during a gruelling session, he stopped and waited for her to catch her breath and give him new instructions.

"It was so therapeutic to be with him again," Karen remembers. "Early on, when it was hard for me to stand, I held on to his mane to support myself and brushed him with my other hand. The more time I spent with him, the more I wanted to do. He motivated me to try things—to carry stuff, brush him, lead him. Physically and emotionally, he really helped to get me going again."

Sometimes when Karen was teaching her beginner students, she sat in her wheelchair at the side of the ring. Each time Merlin passed her he tipped his head toward her and looked at her. He was forever slowing down as he trotted or cantered past. If, at the end of the lesson, the student dropped the reins, he immediately went to Karen and put his head in her lap. "It was great to be at the barn with him, even if I wasn't riding."

Karen's test rides in front of the judges took place during the summer of 2002. Everything went smoothly and she received qualifying scores. She was on the team! Before she knew it, she was packing for a trip to Portugal and the European Championships. One year after breaking her back, Karen Brain was competing for Canada once again.

Portugal

In all this time, Karen had never seen a competition for disabled riders. Ever since she had set herself a new, Para-Equestrian goal, she had been training alone, with no special coaching. She didn't lack confidence about her riding ability; on the contrary, she worried that most of the riders wouldn't have had her years of international experience. She speculated that perhaps the other riders had picked up the sport as part of their therapy and wouldn't have the benefit of her years of lessons and countless hours in the saddle. Karen didn't want to admit it aloud, but she was a little worried that she would be too good. As the team of four Canadian competitors arrived at the show site, she hoped silently that it wasn't too obvious that she was the best rider there. She desperately wanted the competition to be fair.

When the covered arenas came into sight, Karen asked to be let out of the team vehicle. Walking with canes, she

The Canadian team enjoys a carriage ride in Portugal, 2002. From left to right, Jane James, Lauren Barwick, Judi Island, Karen, Jenni Rowe, and Coach Mary Longden up front with the driver.
Photo by Flo Island

made her way over to where some of the competitors were practising. There were some nice-looking horses in the ring—big warmbloods with gorgeous movement. Coaches called out instructions from the ground and, in a couple of cases, able-bodied coaches hopped onto mounts to do a bit of schooling.

One particularly nicely turned-out pair caught Karen's eye. The rider, a young woman, sat very upright and she and the horse, an attractive dark bay, worked beautifully together. "Whose coach is that?" Karen asked another bystander, assuming the disabled rider had yet to mount up.

"That's Angelique," the woman beside her said. "She *is* the rider."

Karen looked at the pair again as they performed a very nice extended trot across the diagonal in the ring. "What's wrong with her?" she asked.

The woman at the rail glanced sideways at Karen and said, "She has no legs."

"What! What grade is she?"

"Two. She's looking very good, isn't she?"

Karen nodded. Way too good. In that moment, all Karen's fears about outclassing the competition evaporated—to be replaced with the sobering thought that she was going to get blown out of the water.

Watching the other riders was an eye-opening experience. There were so many different kinds of disabilities—blind riders, limbless riders, and many with varying degrees of paralysis. One girl without arms needed to hold the reins in her teeth in order to steer. But long before the end of the competition, Karen felt sorry for nobody. These were top-calibre riders on excellent horses. Karen no longer saw the disability but saw only the rider, the person—and her competition. And, she realized, that's how the other coaches and riders saw her.

While there was plenty of camaraderie and hands willing to help if needed, the desire to win was fierce. One of the best Grade 1 riders in the world said to her, "My coach is watching you."

Karen knew what he meant: the team competition requires good riders representing various disability grades. At any point in a competition a rider's designation can be challenged. If a rider is determined to be riding with an incorrect classification, that rider can be eliminated, and if that happened to Karen, the Canadian team would suffer. She squelched her nerves and did what she always did: focused on herself and her horse and the task that lay ahead of them.

Yet another challenge faced the team. For most non-European competitors the cost of transporting a horse overseas was prohibitive, so many riders from nations such as Canada, New Zealand, and Australia had to compete on borrowed horses.

The Canadians used horses owned by the Portuguese military riding team. None was particularly easy to ride—but Karen was used to difficult horses. She rode a captain's horse, Q-Karlos, a lovely mount with whom she got along well.

For a week before the competition started, riders from seventeen nations, particularly those with horses they didn't know, worked hard to polish their tests and refine their Kurs.

Getting ready for a big competition pushes riders to perform at their very best, and the intense work can be hard on both human and equine athletes. The day before the first day of competition, Karen mounted up for a training session and asked her horse to pick up a good working trot. She felt that the horse just wasn't right, and said so. Her coach was reluctant to believe Karen's assessment and insisted they continue with their workout. At the canter, Karen's horse was, disunited and kept breaking into a trot. Karen told her coach that it felt as though the horse was fatigued, unused to the demanding work.

No matter what Karen said, her coach refused to believe that Karen could feel the difference in her mount. It was one of the first times Karen felt put down, that her credibility was being challenged. A small part of her wondered if she would have been disregarded in the same way if she had been an able-bodied rider. The thought was like a dark shadow hovering over her and she fought the urge to burst into tears.

The ride did not end on a good note, and that evening, instead of joining the others for the athletes' banquet following the opening ceremonies, Karen went to her room. The tension between Karen and her coach was only a small part of how low she suddenly felt. It was September 18, 2002—the first anniversary of her accident. An anniversary like this is always tough to get through, all the more so when one is miles away from home without friends and family to offer support. An envelope from home filled with cards and best wishes from everyone somehow made her feel even more alone. Karen's vision blurred and she could hardly read.

Karen's intuition told her that she needed to share some of her unhappiness. The other team members had no idea that she was struggling through her anniversary alone. Hard though it was, she forced herself to leave her room and join the others at the banquet. She arrived just as the teams were

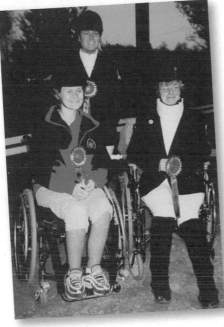

Karen stands behind Lauren Barwick (left) and Judi Island.
Photo by Flo Island

being introduced, and the Canadian athletes walked in together and were welcomed. During the evening she let the others know what was bothering her. Their support was hearty and sincere, and Karen's release was immediate and profound. The team had a fabulous time at the banquet, and Karen was grateful that she had somehow found the strength to come out of her room. The camaraderie and cheerful banter that evening set the tone for the tough competition days that lay ahead. "I never would have guessed that I would come unglued like that," Karen muses. "The other team members probably understood more about what I was going through than I even understood myself."

Over the next several days, all the riders concentrated on their horses and on riding well. When the final scores were tallied, the Canadian team placed seventh overall. Karen realized there had been no need to worry about being the best rider in her division. As an individual, she finished fifth, sixth, and seventh in her various classes. Still, these were the best results for any rider on a borrowed horse, and she was the top Canadian. It was a monumental achievement for a rider who, only three months earlier, had hardly been able to stay in the saddle.

Onward and Upward

Such an astonishing comeback would be enough for many. But Karen had tasted success and she wanted more. She knew she was capable of winning with the right horse and with sufficient preparation. On her return from Portugal, Karen decided she wanted to see just how much of her former riding self she could recover. She was longing to jump again. Would she still have the nerve to pilot a horse around a cross-country course?

Karen met again with her surgeon and received the go-ahead to start jumping. With that vote of confidence she knew she needed to set another goal—to compete at a three-day event. This time it wasn't so important that Karen win. Instead, she would be happy to finish. For that, she would need a partner she could count on.

Merlin hadn't been idle during Karen's convalescence. Although he was retired from top-level competition, a couple of Karen's students had been riding him in lessons. He hadn't been doing any big jumps but was reasonably fit and easily able to handle the lighter work required in lower level riding lessons. Karen knew they both had a lot of work to do before they would be ready to event again. It would be tough for her to fit in the necessary training. Teaching, giving clinics, and continuing an intensive rehabilitation program kept her busy seven days a week.

There were other challenges, physical, financial, and emotional. Walking with her leg braces and two canes, Karen found it hard to cope with Ontario's icy winter conditions. Financial difficulties continued to plague her. She was forced to apply for government assistance but was told that first she had to spend every penny she might have in savings, including even the small amount of money she had received when her grandfather passed away. With her meagre savings gone, and having exhausted every possible source of personal funds, she finally qualified to receive a small disability stipend, barely enough to cover her food and rent. The tangle of paperwork required to obtain this assistance took months, and Karen found the process of having to ask for government help devastating, far worse than anything she had dealt with in terms of her accident and recovery. She felt irrationally guilty every time she had to go to an appointment with her caseworker and often dissolved into tears in the waiting room.

And once again her intensity and independence proved too much for her relationship to bear, and she and Rob parted company. However, neither physical problems, heartbreak, nor the endless grind to earn enough money could hold Karen back. She took time off at Christmas to visit family and friends on Vancouver Island before returning to Ontario to resume her preparations for three-day eventing.

Jumping was particularly difficult with her reduced strength and lingering respiratory problems. Her collapsed lung took months to heal, and even long afterwards she was unable to ride without getting short of breath. Jumping only made this problem worse and drove her to add more aerobic conditioning exercises to her regime.

Karen was especially nervous about jumping cross-country fences, which often require the horse and rider to jump onto or off banks, landing higher or lower than the ground level where they began. For Karen, maintaining a good position in the saddle during these drops meant using muscles that were much weaker than before or even non-functional. Karen wasn't sure if she could keep her feet out in front enough to support her weight on landing.

She began by cantering up and down a natural bank. If she got up enough speed, the horses (she was riding both Merlin and Wink) would jump up onto the rise and off again. "The braver I got, the faster I'd go."

As she built up her confidence, she'd ask the horses to take off from a position farther and farther away in order to get a bigger jump. When she realized she was able to manage, she wanted to do more and more. It was hard on her body, though. The inside of her legs got pinched and her ankles and feet took a beating. Lost muscle mass left her shins bony and vulnerable to being rubbed raw by the stirrup leathers. Between jumping efforts she needed to take plenty of slow walking breaks to rest and reorganize her position. Her back ached when she jumped because she could no longer use the large muscles of her backside to support herself in the two-point position.

But each time she successfully held herself up over a fence she felt proud, determined to get back to where she was before the accident. It became an obsession to event again, to know that she was just as good as she had been before. "It was almost like I was having identity issues. If I wasn't an event rider anymore, then what was I? Would I only ever be a Para rider? Was that good enough?"

In August 2003, Karen entered a Training-level event at Grandview in Ontario to assess how she was doing. By the seventh cross-country fence she was huffing and puffing and drenched in sweat, horrified at how hard it was and thinking only that she could hardly wait until the round was over.

Realizing that the only way to improve was to do more, she fought through the pain, discomfort, and shortness of breath and spent more time riding in her jumping saddle, putting miles on herself and her horse at the canter. She forced herself to hold her two-point position for longer and longer periods, determined to get fitter and stronger. Unable to grip with her legs, Karen relied heavily on her balance and, sometimes, a fistful of mane to stay centred on Merlin's back, even when he was in mid-air over a fence. The shorter stirrups used in jumping were hard on her back, hips, knees, ankles, and feet.

She learned to compensate and continued to keep the worst of the pain at bay with small doses of painkillers.

Karen didn't have a special riding coach to help her figure out how to overcome the new challenges she faced. She analyzed the problems and created solutions herself. Adding the wedge-shaped stirrup treads to her jumping saddle helped reduce the pain and pressure on her weak ankles. Riding without stirrups when she was working on her dressage helped minimize the pain during that phase of training. Each week she grew stronger, more confident, and better able to sustain the effort needed during a long cross-country course.

By this time, Karen rarely used her leg braces and canes for everyday activities. She discovered that lacing up her paddock boots snugly gave her similar support to the leg braces, so she started using them all the time.

Three weeks after the event at Grandview, Karen competed in the Preliminary division at Checkmate Farm in Feversham, Ontario. The worst moment came when she was walking the cross-country course. When she arrived at the water jump complex, she stopped short. The obstacle itself wasn't that difficult and she had no trouble formulating a plan for getting Merlin through it quickly and safely. But when it came time to continue walking to the next fence, Karen was stuck. Her poor balance and weak legs meant she didn't dare hop from one slippery rock to the next like the other riders who had scampered through the creek that fed the water jump. Nor could she make the big step up and over a wide gap to a small footbridge.

Another group of riders caught up to her and Karen pretended to be analyzing the obstacle, too embarrassed to admit that she couldn't get herself across. They moved on and Karen paced up and down at the edge of the water, unable to figure out a way to get across the water without injuring herself. Exasperated, Karen muttered, "If you can't *walk* the course, how are you supposed to ride it?"

A second group of riders, including her old coach Peter Gray and various other peers, approached the water jump. The riders exchanged pleasantries, then analyzed their options and continued on to the rest of the course. Karen didn't want to ask for help—she didn't want anyone to feel sorry for her or to think she didn't belong in the competition. Though generally one to focus on the positive, Karen had a bleak flash of realization. "It was one of those moments when I fully understood what it was to be disabled."

Finally, Karen waited until the coast was clear, flung herself forward, and caught the footbridge with her arms. Somehow she hauled herself up, using the strength in her arms and upper body to drag herself to safety.

When Karen and Merlin hit the cross-country course, Karen didn't push her horse for speed—at Merlin's age he wasn't really in contention for top honours. But Karen needed to know that she could do it, that she could come back to eventing if she really wanted to. Her successful rounds proved that.

Two weeks later, Karen and Merlin went on to compete at another Preliminary event at Glen Oro in Ontario. On the cross-country course, Merlin felt soft; he wasn't pulling and eager to run as he had been in the past. "I almost pulled him up halfway around and retired on course," Karen recalls.

Karen finished the course, but she knew even before the final fence that Merlin had reached the end of his eventing career. Karen gave her wonderful black horse a huge hug and officially retired him from the jumping world. He had stepped up to the plate one last time. She wouldn't ask him again.

As for her own return to the eventing world, it took some time before Karen acknowledged that, physically, she was now limited as a jump jockey. "It took time to admit to myself that I would never go to the World Championships or the Olympics as an event rider. It took time to admit that to myself and even longer to say it out loud to other people." The process of letting go of what had become part of her identity was hard. "It felt like I was copping out, taking an easy excuse not to do the tough sport anymore."

She continued to struggle with the question of whether or not Para competition would be enough to satisfy her fierce drive. "Then I said to myself, 'Do the Para competition until you get beyond the top level of competition available. Then go for the Olympic dressage team.'" This shift in perspective made all the difference. Setting the long-term goal of the national dressage team "made not eventing okay because I would still be able to pursue my Olympic dream."

She might have retired her horse from high-level competition, but Karen herself was just getting started.

8

The Road to Athens

Karen and Merlin in 2006. Photo by Nikki Tate

BY EARLY 2004, Karen was ready to rejoin the Canadian Para-Equestrian dressage team and do whatever it took to participate in the Paralympic Games in Athens.

Her place on the team was not guaranteed, because she had not competed at the World Championships in 2003. Instead, following her successful showing in Portugal, she had chosen to focus on herself and her personal goal of competing again as an eventer. Nevertheless, Karen's riding was getting better all the time and she was now a serious contender for a medal in Athens—if she made the team.

To achieve the best possible final team of four riders, the selection criteria were changed three times during the months leading up to the Games. The selection process dragged on for months, and up until the last minute, riders did not know whether they would be travelling to Athens or not. During one round of protests and counter-arguments, fifteen people—including lawyers, riders, representatives from Equine Canada, the national team coaching staff, selection committee members, and Karen—spent nearly six hours in a gruelling conference call debating the merits of a challenge to the decision to include Karen on the team. Riders who had lost their place on the team demanded to know why they had been dropped and whether the shows Karen had ridden at were appropriate for contributing her qualifying scores.

Karen found the process of defending herself and her position on the team exhausting. But in the end, on July 24, she received word that she would be one of the riders going to the Paralympic Games in Athens in September. The others were Lauren Barwick and Dax Adam (both Grade II athletes) and Judi Island (Grade I).

Just three days later, Karen flew to Germany to meet with one of the world's top dressage coaches, Conrad Schumacher, and his assistant, Ellen Bontje, who would help Karen prepare for the Games. Some of her costs were covered by government funds provided to national team members, but Karen, her family, and the other team athletes also took part in ongoing fundraising efforts. Even though more than a hundred businesses and individuals made contributions to Karen's fund, the total from all sources was still not enough to cover all her expenses. To finance the balance of her travel, accommodations, lessons, horse board, and horse lease fees, Karen used her credit cards.

Karen's next challenge was to find a horse to ride, a formidable task at such a late date. Without knowing for certain if she was going to be on the team, she had been able to make only tentative inquiries from Canada. She had contacted many people in the European horse world but her

123

What Makes Dressage So Hard?

To the uninitiated, dressage looks deceptively simple. Even during the most complex tests at the highest levels of international competitions, it seems as if the rider sits very still and stays relaxed while the horse magically speeds up, slows down, pirouettes, prances sideways, and dances on the spot.

The truth is, communication between rider and horse is constant and exacting, and it must also be silent. The rider uses subtle shifts of body weight and position, slight adjustments of rein tightness, and constant changes of leg position and pressure to indicate the direction the horse should move, the speed of that movement, and the gait the horse should use. Transitions from canter to trot or walk may be cued by a slight tightening of the muscles in the seat and lower back. Horses must also learn to collect and extend (shorten and lengthen) their stride on command without changing the cadence or rhythm of their gait. At all times the horse must be soft, supple, and obedient and must move smoothly from one movement to the next, one gait to another.

While the rider is constantly "speaking" to the horse through the hands, seat, back, legs, and shifts of weight, the horse is also speaking back to the rider. A hesitation in stride might mean the horse has momentarily lost balance or is uncertain what the rider has asked (the rider's cues, though subtle, must be crystal clear). Leaning (pulling) against the bit or tossing the head might be a way of avoiding the rider's aids (cues). A swishing tail might mean the horse is feeling cranky or uncomfortable. Resistance to the aids, as by being slow to move away from a leg touching one side of the horse, might mean the horse is tired, hasn't had a long enough warm-up, or is being asked to do work that is too difficult. A good rider knows how to read the messages the horse is sending—what it means when a horse's ears are cocked back slightly and tuned in to the rider as opposed to pinned back (a sign of irritation or aggression) or pricked forward and focused on something outside the ring.

It takes years of training for the horse and hundreds of hours in the saddle for the rider before they learn to speak the same language, and the longer a particular pair spends together, the better they become at this interspecies communication. No two horses respond to a rider's aids in the same way, and no two riders ride in exactly the same way.

A dressage competition involves tests of set elements as well as the Kurs, freestyle dressage tests set to music in which the rider is allowed to combine elements in any order. At each level of competition, certain movements are mandatory. At any given competition—whether a local training show, where horses execute very simple patterns at the walk and trot, or an elite event such as the Olympic Games—riders may ride several tests. It can be tricky to remember what comes next when several tests have been memorized!

Internationally, the tests are standardized by the FEI, with the top levels called Prix Saint George, Intermediate I, Intermediate II, and Grand Prix. Olympic riders must complete a Grand Prix test while top Paralympic riders do a Para-Equestrian version of the slightly less complex Prix Saint George test.

With the incredible stress and excitement of competing at a large international competition, the difficulties of riding what is often a borrowed horse, and the fundamental challenges of dressage tests themselves, it's not hard to see just how difficult it is to produce an excellent score at an event like the Paralympic Games.

Karen schooling her mare, VDL Odelle, at the canter in Saanichton, 2006.

list of possibilities was awfully short. Owners of top horses were unwilling to hold them if a rider couldn't guarantee she would be competing. Several excellent prospects had been promised to other riders during the time Canada was still finalizing the team roster.

One of the possible mounts she had heard about belonged to a Belgian family. After arriving in Europe, Karen made arrangements to travel to see him. Otis, a dark bay 16 hh Thoroughbred, was a former eventer, and Karen was hopeful that he might be suitable.

When Karen arrived in Belgium, the family was extremely kind. Unfortunately, after riding Otis, Karen had serious doubts that she would be able to get him to perform the higher level movements required in Athens. She said as much in a frantic phone call to the Canadian chef d'équipe, Jane James. The advice she received was to take the horse to Germany to let Conrad do a full assessment. Karen knew that wasn't going to help, but with no other prospects, she agreed.

Karen and Otis returned to Germany a week later. Conrad looked the horse over and declared, "I'm happy that you found a good horse." Karen wasn't so sure.

The lessons began immediately. A few days later, after Karen finished her warm-up with Otis, she started doing some more advanced movements—canter half-pass, flying changes, and counter canter. At one point in the lesson, Conrad asked her to come down the centre line and then do a canter half-pass. Otis spun off to the right, whirling in a tight circle.

"What is *that*?" Conrad asked. Karen gritted her teeth. *That* was an example of why the horse wasn't going to work out. "Do not kick him this time," Conrad instructed.

"I didn't kick him!" Karen protested silently, not daring to say anything out loud.

She repeated the manoeuvre and the horse spun sideways again, taking off like a racehorse with his head in the air.

Reversing directions, Karen tried again. Coming off the left rein the horse was a little better, but still not wonderful.

"Tomorrow, Ellen will ride the horse," Conrad said after the lesson.

Karen's heart dropped to her boots. She had promised the Belgian family that under no circumstances would she let anyone else ride the horse. But how could she say no to Conrad? He was her coach and he needed to know what kind of horse he was working with. Ellen was a top-notch rider with years of experience. Still, the thought of anyone else getting on Otis ate away at Karen.

The next day, Karen took the horse through a long, slow warm-up. Then Ellen mounted. Conrad spoke to Ellen in German. Ellen asked Otis for the same movement that had caused Karen so much grief the day before. Sure enough, the horse tried to rear and then spun off to the right, bolting sideways.

"At least we know it's not you," Conrad remarked dryly to Karen. It was a bittersweet moment. Karen did feel vindicated that she had not done something to annoy the horse, but it didn't bode well for her Paralympic prospects that the horse was so reactive.

Ellen had plenty to say to Conrad in German as she rode past. Conrad translated for Karen. "Ellen doesn't like the horse. Ellen says the horse is not good enough. Do you have to ride this horse?"

Karen shrugged. "He's all I have." Then she ventured, "Do you have anything here that might be suitable?"

The stern dressage master looked at his new pupil and answered, "We do not have horses for rent here."

Karen's heart sank. This wasn't going the way she had hoped. It was nearly the middle of August—time was running out!

She wondered if Conrad was going to send her home. He had said all along that he couldn't help her if she didn't have a decent horse. If this one wasn't good enough, was she going to be kicked out of Conrad's barn and sent back to Canada without ever setting foot in Athens? She racked her brains, trying to think of some way to fly Merlin to Europe in time to compete: surely her old partner wouldn't let her down. But there was not enough time, and in any case he had been out of training for this level of competition for too long.

Later that day, Ellen found Karen and said, to her surprised relief, "Tomorrow we go and look at horses."

The next day, Karen tried not to show how excited she was. But it was tough to contain herself—she was thrilled to have a chance to see what some of the top barns in Germany had to offer. "It was a bit like turning a kid loose in a toy shop," Karen says. "I loved being able to try those amazing horses."

When Ellen and Karen set out on their horse-hunting mission, Karen did everything she could think of to make the time they spent together in the car pleasant. Ellen was not a particularly chatty person, but Karen was nervous, wanting to make a good impression. She asked a lot of questions about the finer points of dressage and riding at the Grand Prix level. "Some day I'd like to ride Grand Prix. I'd like to do all those fancy tricks."

Ellen didn't say anything, but Karen later learned that calling the complex and subtle movements of the highest level of dressage "fancy tricks" was one of Ellen's pet peeves.

Oblivious, Karen chatted on. She asked how many paint horses there were in the Grand Prix circuit.

"None," Ellen answered.

"I always wanted a paint warmblood," Karen went on.

Ellen shot her a disdainful look.

"What?" Karen said.

Ellen launched into a long explanation about how the markings make the horses look as if they are moving unevenly, even if they aren't. Karen had the distinct feeling she wasn't exactly making a new friend. Later that day, Ellen waved her hand at a field and said, "Look! A herd of paint warmbloods."

Karen squinted at the collection of black and white animals. "Ellen! Those are cows!" She began to suspect that Ellen might have a sense of humour after all.

When it came time to look at horses, Ellen was all business. She and Karen tried several prospects but in each case had reservations about how suitable the horse would be. After Ellen conversed in German with someone at another barn they visited, a horse was brought out. Ellen and Karen watched someone else ride, and the horse looked as if it was moving well and was reasonably obedient. Then Karen had a ride. Ellen didn't say too much but watched closely. She instructed Karen to sit the trot and ask for some collection.

"Not so fast!" She tapped her whip—tap-tap-tap. "There, that rhythm is your passage." She tapped again. "There— your piaffe."

As Ellen called out instructions and made suggestions, Karen understood just how solidly the other woman stood behind her. She grew more confident that they would find the right horse for the job.

The next horse they saw was a mare called Dasskara, Donna for short. Watching another rider put her through her paces, they agreed the mare looked harder to ride.

Karen mounted up and to her surprise found that she and the horse got along very well. Karen asked and the horse responded and soon they were working well together. Karen found it easier to sit Donna's trot, and when they moved on to some canter work the mare did exactly what she was told, even giving Karen flying changes when asked.

"Ellen!" Karen called as they flew past. "I love her!"

Ellen nodded. With a cheeky grin Karen added, "Do you have her in a paint version?"

After the riding trial was over and Dasskara had been led away, the trainer beckoned to Ellen. Karen asked if she should give them some time alone to discuss the possibility of using the horse in Athens. "Sit down," Ellen said. "If we want to talk about you we'll do it in German."

Dasskara was owned by an American and there was considerable discussion back and forth about the likelihood of the mare being

Karen's athlete identification badge from the Athens Paralympic Games in 2004. Like many athletes, Karen enjoys collecting pins.

available through September, and the best way to approach the owner to secure the use of the horse. A lease fee of several thousand dollars was agreed upon and Karen was given the go-ahead to use the horse for the necessary time. With permission obtained and Dasskara moved to Conrad's barn, Karen was thrilled to find herself again riding under Conrad's watchful eye, this time on a horse she knew she would be able to ride well.

After about three weeks of training together, Karen and Dasskara were ready. At her going-away party, Karen received many warm wishes, cards, and genuinely friendly hugs.

Through tears Karen said, "Thank you so much for finding Donna."

Ellen replied, "Good luck. You are always welcome to come back here."

Donna was shipped to Athens and Karen left the next day, with Conrad following a week later.

9

A Dream Comes True

Canada's Paralympic riders and support team
in Athens, 2004. Karen is second from the
right, standing.

"Yogurt and Scheisse"

THE CANADIAN TEAM AND ITS MOUNTS arrived ten days
before the first competition day. Despite the pressures and
stresses of the imminent competition, Karen felt a deep inner
calm during the training sessions leading up to the opening
day. She had a strong feeling that she would do well and
would medal at the Games.

In the weeks before the Games, Karen had several powerful
dreams. In one she saw herself on the medal podium. In
another she saw herself standing fourth in line as the last
rider. This second dream didn't make sense since the dream

about the medal had been so strong and crystal clear. She remembered seeing the number "69," but when Karen arrived at the barns, she learned that Donna's stall number was 404. She had a moment of doubt when she wondered about the accuracy of her dreams—if her stall number was wrong, was her final placing also wrong? But there was no confusing the image of a medal hung around her neck. Medals were not handed out to fourth-place finishers.

On the morning of September 20, Karen prepared to ride a warm-up test in front of the same judges who would see her ride in three additional tests over the course of the week. Well in advance of her four o'clock ride time, she made her way to the barn to find Donna standing in the back of her stall with her head down. "How's Donna?" she asked the Canadian team groom.

The Paralympic Games

The Paralympic Games are held every four years in association with, and usually after, the Olympic Games. The idea of athletics for disabled participants originated in England in 1948 when Sir Ludwig Guttman, a neurologist, organized a competition for some of his patients. Many were Second World War veterans who had suffered various kinds of spinal cord injuries during the war. Guttman's patients competed against patients from other hospitals.

In 1960, four hundred wheelchair athletes competed in Rome, and the term "Paralympics" (from Parallel Olympics) was coined. With the exception of 1980 (when the Soviet Union refused to host the Paralympic Games and disabled athletes from forty-two countries competed at an alternate venue in Holland), the Paralympics have been held in association with the Olympic Games ever since. The Paralympic Games are now the second-largest sporting event in the world.

Over the years, the range of disabilities included has broadened and the number of sports has increased. Equestrian competition was added to the roster in Atlanta in 1996. In Sydney, Australia, in 2000, 132 nations took part in the Paralympic Games, and in Athens, 2004, more than 3,800 athletes from 136 countries competed in nineteen sports. The Athens Paralympics were held from September 17 to September 28, 2004.

"Fine."

Karen went back to the stall to find Donna lying down. The mare looked back at her side and groaned. "She's not fine! She's sick! We have to get her on her feet!" Karen said, rushing into the mare's stall.

Karen and the groom got Donna up, took her out of the stall, and started leading her around. Within minutes the horse was crippled with pain and could hardly walk. Spasms rippled the muscles of her stomach, and her back bunched up with cramps.

Karen called the vet and was relieved to see Conrad, who had appeared just minutes after Karen had forced Donna to her feet and sent the groom to walk her. The mare was now in agony and seemed about to collapse. Urging her to stay on her feet and keep moving, the group managed to get the mare to the emergency clinic. Conrad let the Canadian chef d'équipe know that Karen needed to cancel her warm-up ride, and the show officials were notified of the crisis.

Debate raged as to what to do to help the distressed horse. A tranquilizer was out of the question, as were traditional drugs given for colic. The mare wasn't allowed to compete with anti-inflammatory drugs in her system. As they watched, the mare's belly became distended with gas. Conrad phoned Germany and asked for a complete medical history on the mare. With few options available, the crew took turns walking Donna slowly back and forth, hoping to gently loosen the blockage in her gut. She was dosed with the maximum amount of a legal muscle relaxant to try to ease her discomfort, and an iv drip was hooked up so she could receive fluids. Heated opinions were expressed over the point at which it was going to be necessary to administer powerful (but illegal in competition) drugs and pull out of the Games. In consultation with vets and team officials, the decision was made to give the mare a little more time to see if she could work through the colic with alternative treatments.

After nearly two hours, Donna passed a little wind, a good sign.

Intense discussions continued. Finally, Conrad told Karen, "The vet will put in a stomach tube and give her yogurt and scheisse."

Karen is not impressed with the smell of the mixture about to be pumped into Dasskara's stomach! Also in the photo is Helen Ford (groom) and one of the vets who treated Dasskara in Athens, 2004.

With the conversation going on in a mixture of German, heavily accented English, and Greek, Karen wasn't sure she had understood.

"Pardon?" she asked.

Conrad repeated himself distractedly while directing an assistant to get supplies.

Though Karen thought she knew what *scheisse* meant, it didn't make any sense to her that someone would feed manure to a horse. Maybe it was German slang, a casual reference to some mixture of approved drugs or herbs. Not wanting to seem stupid, Karen gave

Karen holds Dasskara while a vet administers a mixture of horse manure and yogurt.

up trying to find out exactly what was going to be pumped into the mare's already upset stomach.

Before long, the assistant was back with yogurt that was poured into a big bucket. This actually was mixed with manure from a healthy horse to make a sticky soup. Wide-eyed, Karen watched as the nasty-smelling mixture was pumped into Dasskara's stomach. When she asked how they had come up with this remedy, the vet explained that the active bacteria in the yogurt along with the healthy flora in the other horse's manure would help restore the proper balance of bacteria in Donna's gut.

Amazingly, the treatment worked. Before long, Donna was passing wind—lots of it—and then manure. As her gut began working properly again, she perked right up, though she still smelled terrible, as if she had eaten rotten eggs.

To help the mare's delicate digestive system, the team switched her to plain grass hay. It seemed she simply couldn't handle the rich alfalfa hay the other horses were being fed.

Donna improved quickly enough that, two days later, Karen was able to ride her horse in a lovely collected trot around the outside perimeter of the dressage ring as her first test began.

Against all odds, Karen Brain was about to ride at the Paralympic Games in Athens, Greece.

Precision and Grace

In June 2004, Karen had been reclassified as a Grade IV athlete. Able to walk quite well without canes as long as the footing was not too uneven, Karen took simple precautions such as always wearing boots that extended above the ankle, or, if she wore sandals, also using a short brace on her left leg. She still found it hard to position her legs correctly when she rode—they tended to slip too far forward. Her leg muscles were much weaker than an able-bodied rider's, so

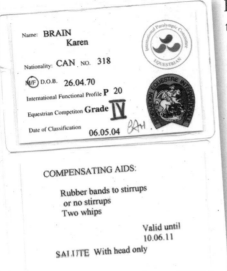

Karen was permitted to carry two dressage whips and use special elastics to keep her feet in the stirrups (though she has never actually used the elastics). Because her hands were full with the reins and whips, Karen was also permitted to salute the judge using only her head rather than giving the traditional salute in which the rider drops one arm down to her side. These details are clearly stated on the back of Karen's rider identification card.

But none of these details mattered to Karen as the familiar adrenaline rush of competition — never before so strong — washed over her.

This is it, she thought. *I'm at the Paralympic Games…about to go into the ring…this is what I've worked so hard for!* But right away Karen squelched her delight and refocused. "Turn it off," she said sharply to herself. "Get into work mode."

Conrad had coached her that the good riders show off a little on the outside of the ring, hoping to impress the judges before the official start of the test. "I loved Dasskara and I knew she looked good," Karen recalls of her lap around the outside of the ring. "I remember telling myself not to get carried away, not to get too emotional or dreamy. The next six minutes would determine whether or not I'd win a medal."

The electronic chime sounded and, as ready as she would ever be, Karen turned her horse up the centre line of the dressage ring in a fine collected trot. She halted and bowed her head in a formal salute to the judges.

With intense concentration, Karen and Donna methodically executed the twenty-five movements required in the FEI Para-Equestrian Grade IV Individual Championship Test. They circled to the left and right, collected and extended at the walk, trot, and canter, moved sideways, and performed half-pirouettes at the walk.

With each circle, change of gait or direction, extension, or collection, Karen heard Conrad's voice in her head—"Keep her in front of your leg! Don't let her drift!" As she put it later, "I know that when Conrad is watching, he can see everything that I feel."

In the audience, Karen's family hardly breathed as Karen worked her way through the test. Judges told scribes seated beside them a score and a comment for each movement. The judges' eyes never left the horse and rider. At the side of the ring, Conrad studied every movement in the test as intently as any of the judges.

As Karen completed each movement, the judges' scores flashed up on the big electronic scoreboard. Once, Karen caught herself glancing at the board and immediately snapped at herself, "What are you doing? Focus!"

After the final movement, Karen and Donna halted to salute and then left the ring. As they walked out, two sets of emotions and thoughts battled in Karen. The perfectionist in

her was already analyzing all the tiny errors she felt she had made. Her optimistic side, though,

Karen and Dasskara during the Individual Championship Dressage Test in Athens, 2004.

was ready to weep with the thrill of having ridden a good test on a lovely horse at the highest level of competition.

Karen's score proved good enough to earn her third place—a bronze medal and the top finish for a rider on a borrowed horse.

Karen's mother, Darlene Brain, and coach, Conrad Schumacher, in the stands in Athens, 2004. Photo by Terri Gold

It's hard to say who was prouder or more excited—Karen, receiving a traditional crown of olive leaves and feeling the weight of her medal around her neck, or her

family, in tears in the stands. Karen could not have been happier with Donna—when she saw the level of competition in Athens she knew in her heart that Merlin would not have been competitive with the highly bred dressage specialists in the ring.

Reaching the medal podium would not have been possible without the support of a loving family. Karen and her sister, Terri Gold, are all smiles in Athens, 2004.

As she sat on her horse while her medal was presented, she felt profoundly grateful to the mare who had come so far with her in such a short time. As they left the ring, the atmosphere was electric. The sensitive mare picked up on the excitement and began to piaffe and passage, appearing to dance as they left the ring.

"The horse felt great," she remembers, "and I secretly hoped I would medal again so I could experience Donna's sense of excitement again."

Conrad was thrilled with Karen's efforts, so excited for her that he could hardly contain his enthusiasm.

Two days later, on September 24, Karen rode her second test, the Kur. Her performance included a half-pass ridden in a zigzag pattern, flying changes, ten-metre circles in both directions, and extension and collection at all three gaits. Set to the music "I'm in Heaven," the Kur was a big success, once again netting Karen an excellent score—and a second bronze medal! Karen's face broke into a

Karen and Dasskara in Athens, 2004.

A note in Karen's scrapbook thanking her many supporters.

Thank you so much to every one who has helped me in so many ways,
With your emotional support along the way,
Financial support, phone calls,
Emails, fundraising, etc.
I couldn't have done it without you!!!
Thank you!!!
xoxooxxoo

huge grin when the announcer's voice spoke her name and she watched the Canadian flag flutter in the breeze.

Back at the Athlete's Village, when Karen had her medals engraved with her name and the name of her horse, she asked the engravers how busy they had been.

"We're much busier now than we were after the regular Olympics," they told her. "So many of the athletes want something engraved on their medals!"

Karen nodded and her eyes brimmed with tears as she realized why that was. "Every athlete who wins a medal at the Paralympic Games has had to overcome so much. It's hard for other people to know just how much those medals mean to us."

The route Karen Brain had taken to the podium may not have been the one imagined by her nine-year-old self, but despite all the challenges along the way, she had achieved her childhood dream.

Two bronze medals—the reward after a lifetime of hard work.

Epilogue

Photo by Nikki Tate

The Road to Beijing

Karen's third dressage test in Athens was in the team competition. Though her score of 70.42 percent was high enough to rank her second overall, Canadian Paralympic team member Judi Island was unable to compete following an earlier fall from her horse. As a result, the Canadian team did not have a fourth rider and the chance to drop the lowest score. Their overall team average placed the Canadian team ninth.

Since Karen's double-medal performance in Athens, she has continued to ride, competing successfully for the Canadian Para-Equestrian team in England, Belgium, and the Netherlands as well as at home in Canada. She has received qualifying scores for Beijing and is once again in contention for a spot on the team Canada will send to China to compete at the Paralympic Games in 2008. The equestrian events will be held in Hong Kong. Karen is training a new horse, vdl Odette, and is working with Conrad Schumacher in Germany to hone her skills further so she'll be ready to take on the world.

Beyond 2008, Karen has her eye on the World Equestrian Games in Kentucky in 2010 and, if all goes according to plan, a place on Canada's Olympic dressage team. Competing against able-bodied riders at the Olympic Games is still one of Karen's dreams. Anyone who has met Karen Brain can't help feeling it is only a matter of time before this remarkable athlete and committed horsewoman stands on the podium and holds her Olympic medal high.

To follow Karen's career, and to learn more about how to support national team athletes, visit www.karenbrain.ca.

Karen and VDL Odette compete at a dressage show at the Saanich Fairgrounds in 2006.
Photo by Nikki Tate

Glossary

aids (leg aids, riding aids). The instructions the rider gives to the horse using seat, legs, hands, and voice.

bank (n). A type of obstacle on a cross-country course for which the takeoff and landing are on different levels of ground. Sometimes banks must be jumped in sequence in a stair-like configuration.

bank (v). Horses may touch down on top of or push off from a solid cross-country jump. This is known as "banking" the obstacle.

bay. A dark brown horse with black points (the mane, tail, and lower legs).

canter. A three-beat gait faster than a trot and slower than a gallop.

carded athlete. An athlete who is competing successfully at an international level receives a special designation from the sport's governing organization and is then eligible to receive financial assistance and access to certain services.

cavaletti. A small jump, typically a single pole fastened between two x-shaped supports. The height can be changed by rolling the jump over.

chef d'équipe. The team manager responsible for logistics during international competition.

collection. The compressing or shortening of a horse's frame and stride accomplished by lightening the forehand and taking more weight on the hindquarters.

coop jump. A jumping obstacle made of two panels fastened together at the top and angled out at the bottom.

counter canter. A canter in which the horse leads with the outside pair of legs instead of the inside pair, as is more usual.

diagonal. See **posting diagonal.**

disunited. Horses canter and gallop with either their left or their right legs leading, usually depending on their direction of travel (the legs on the inside of a circle will come forward first and reach farther ahead). A horse that is disunited canters or gallops with one front leg and the opposite hind leg leading.

dressage. From the French word meaning "training," dressage is simply a traditional way of riding and training a horse to move in a balanced, controlled, and supple manner.

flatwork. Schooling without jumping exercises.

flying changes. Shifting from one canter lead to the other without a transition through the trot.

hack class. A class in a horse show without a jumping element. Ridden on the flat, horses are typically asked to walk, trot, canter, halt, and back up under saddle. Horses are judged on their suitability for riding.

half-pass. A dressage movement in which the horse travels forward and sideways at the same time. This can be done at all three gaits (walk, trot, and canter).

hand. Standard measure of horse height equal to 4 inches (10.2 centimetres). A horse measuring 15 hands high (15 hh) is 5 feet or 1.52 metres tall at the withers.

hunter-jumper. Show-ring jumping classes are divided into two categories: hunter and jumper. In hunter classes, the emphasis is on a smooth, steady ride with the horse maintaining a rhythmic gait from start to end of the course. Hunters are judged subjectively based on factors such as style, overall impression, and way of going. Jumper classes focus on speed and accuracy. It doesn't matter how a horse looks; the only criterion for doing well is clearing all the fences faster than other competitors. The horse and rider with the fewest jumping faults wins the class.

jump standards. The posts or stands used to support the ends of the poles or planks of a horse jump.

long-listed athlete. A competitor who has been identified as having competitive potential and is in contention for a place on a team.

oxer. A type of horse jump that includes two sets of rails. The rails may be set at the same level, or the front or back rail may be higher. The most difficult type of oxer is called a "square oxer," a fence that is as high as it is wide.

passage. A trot where the horse seems to be moving in slow motion because of a longer moment of suspension between steps and a higher lift as the opposite foreleg and hind leg move forward in unison.

piaffe. A very collected trot in which the horse does not move forward at all.

pluggy. Refers to a slow-moving, quiet, or placid horse.

pony. A horse under 14.2 hh.

posting diagonal. When a horse is trotting, the rider rises and sits in time to the horse's rhythm. This action is called posting. To remain in balance with the horse (particularly when turning), the rider must rise out of the saddle as the inside hind leg comes forward under the horse. An easy way to check this is to watch the horse's outside shoulder—as it comes forward, the rider should be rising. When rising at the correct time, the rider is said to be on the correct diagonal.

run-out. A horse avoiding a fence by ducking off to the side rather than jumping over the obstacle.

short-listed athlete. A rider who has qualified by obtaining strong results in approved competitions and who therefore has a good chance of being invited to join a team.

splint bone. The main bone in the lower leg of a horse is called the cannon bone. The two smaller bones on either side of the cannon bone, attached by a ligament, are the splint bones.

trot. A two-beat running gait in which the foreleg and hind leg on opposite sides of the body move forward in unison.

two-point position. The position used for jumping or galloping, in which the rider's body is raised up out of the saddle, leaving only two points of contact with the horse's body (the rider's legs).

walk-trot classes. Horse show classes in which no canter work is required. Typically, these classes are offered for less-experienced horses and/or riders.

warmblood. Traditionally, horses were referred to as being cold-blooded (draft horses) or hot-blooded (Arabians and Thoroughbreds). Warmblood breeds were originally developed as all-around riding, driving, agricultural, and military horses and may have bloodlines from either category. Today, warmbloods excel in many areas of equestrian sport. In order to be registered or approved, warmbloods must meet performance standards. Different warmblood breeds are named for the regions in which their respective stud books (breeding records) are maintained (e.g., Irish Sport Horse, Hanoverian, or Dutch, Danish, or Swedish warmbloods).

withers. The ridge between the shoulder bones of a horse.

Index

Brain, Karen.
    Alpo
        buys 35
        sells 50–54
    appeal of eventing 37, 43, 64, 66
    B.C. Combined Training high-point ribbon (1986) 40
    breaks back in fall *15*, 81–84
        anniversary of accident 114–15
        collapsed lung 86
        moves her toes 92–93
        physiotherapy 89–90, 91, 93, 95–97, 100–101, *103*
        relief after accident 94–95
        returns to eventing 116, 117–21
        riding after accident 97–98, 103–6, 108, 109–10
        surgery 85–87
    buys first horse 24–25
    Canadian eventing team 64–65, 67
    depression after selling Alpo 50–54
    employment
        barn jobs 20, 24, 35, 37, 43, 54, 67
        riding instruction 42, 61, 67, 102, 109, 116
        non-horse jobs 109
    European Championships for Disabled Riders (2002) 111–15
    family support 20, 24, 37, 39–40, 42, 95, *100, 139*
    finances 24, 35, 42, 53, 61, 67–68, 123
    financial difficulties 39–40, 61, 116–17
    future plans 143
    Matzi
        buys 60–61
        sells 76–77
    Merlin
        buys 55
        bowed tendon 74–76
        retires 120
    Miko 79–81, *86*
    moves east 43, 61–62
    North American Young Riders Championship (1988) 44

eventing *(continued)*
   levels 36
   vet inspections 71

F

Fair Hill cci*** (1997) 66, *67*
Far Hill event (1988) 45
Fédération Equestre Internationale (FEI) 59
   dressage 125
   event rating 59
Flynn, Bridget 34
Ford, Helen *135*
Freeman Farms Preliminary Championship 57, *58*

G

Gatcombe Park 45–46
Gatwick Horse Trials (1989) 46, *46*
Glen Oro
   cci* (2000) 79
   Horse Trials (1999) 76
   Preliminary event (2003) 120
Gleneagles Riding School 45–46
Gold, Rob (Karen's brother-in-law) 60–61, 76–77
Grandview (2003) 118
Gray, Peter 61, 65, 72, 78, 120
Guttman, Ludwig 133

H

Hart, Emily 71
Hatt, Laura 63
Holmes-Smith, Nick 43, 58–59
Horse Trials B.C. 40
horse trials. *See* eventing
Howard, Jenny *20*
Hunt Valley 54

I

incomplete paraplegia 87

Southern Pines
   1997 event 64
   2000 event 77
spinal cord injury 82–83, 87, 91, 94, 102, 105
Spring Ridge Farm 29
Spruce Meadows (1995) *60*
stadium jumping. *See* show jumping
steeplechase (in eventing) 27
Swartz Bay ferry terminal 38–39

T

three-day events. *See* eventing
Todd, Mark 46

V

Vandy 20, 22
VDL Odette *26, 125, 142, 143*

W

Webster, Carol 20
Whidbey Island three-day event (1994) 28
Wink *105*, 109, 117
World Equestrian Games (1998) 67, 70
   event rating 59

Y

Young, Alan 69, 74, 78